Spiritual Warfare

Michael Harper

SERVANT BOOKS
Ann Arbor, Michigan

Copyright © 1970, 1984 by Michael Harper
All rights reserved

Published with revisions in 1984 by Servant Books,
   P.O. Box 8617, Ann Arbor, Michigan 48107

Cover photo by John B. Leidy © 1984 Servant Publications
Book and cover design by John B. Leidy

        90   10 9 8 7

Scripture quotations are taken from the New English Bible, New
Testament © 1961, by permission of Oxford and Cambridge
Universities Presses.

Library of Congress Catalog Card Number 71-135048

Printed in the United States of America
ISBN 0-89283-175-8

SPIRITUAL WARFARE

By the Same Author

Live by the Spirit
The Love Affair
Let My People Grow

Contents

Introduction

THE EARLY CHRISTIANS often seem to have viewed their experience in terms of warfare. Military terminology is liberally sprinkled through the pages of the New Testament. Faith was "the good fight." Protection was seen in terms of "the armour of God." The word of God is likened to "a sword." Satan's attacks are "fiery darts."

Although the Mediterranean nations were enjoying at this time what came to be known as the *Pax Romana*, these lands were garrisoned by Roman soldiers, giving a military atmosphere to the whole of life.

But the war the Christians talked about was not "against flesh and blood." The weapons they wielded were not "carnal." It was spiritual warfare. It was a battle against "the spiritual hosts of wickedness in the heavenly places." And that is what this book is all about.

We too live in a world dominated by military powers. But Christians must also focus on the spiritual warfare which lies behind it. It will increase as the end of the age draws nearer, and Christ's return becomes imminent. The basic New Testament principles of spiritual warfare remain the same, even though Satan dresses himself up in new disguises.

In the preface of C.S. Lewis' masterly exposure of this spiritual warfare, *The Screwtape Letters,* he expresses the hope that his book would not get into the hands of "ill-disposed and excitable people." I hope this book will be spared that fate also. There are always those who use Satan as a kind of scapegoat for their own failings. But there is a more sinister aberration than this. The Pharisees were jealous of Jesus and accused Him of being a satanic agent and even of having a demon. So there are those who see evil in others, which is really often a projection of their own. May God preserve us from such people.

There are a number of references in this book to what is generally called today "spiritualism." This word has been used rather than "spiritism," which more correctly describes it, since it is the one in more common use.

Finally I should like to thank a number of people who took the trouble to read the original manuscript and who made so many helpful comments and criticisms.

I

War Declared!

Now war arose in heaven.
Rev. 12:7

ONE

A Time of Troubles

*You must face the facts: the final age of this world is to be a
time of troubles.* 2 Tim. 3:1 NEB

IN NOVEMBER 1965 the Fountain Trust invited the Rev. Dennis
Bennett to Britain from the United States. In a very full
programme he spoke at many meetings. He was the rector of an
Episcopal church in Seattle, which became famous at the
beginning of the charismatic renewal. This is a reviving work of
the Holy Spirit which is transforming small churches like St.
Luke's into dynamic centres of power, influencing and affecting
the lives of many. St. Luke's had sunk so low, there was only one
way to go—upwards.

It was a very foggy night for one of Mr. Bennett's meetings,
but in spite of the conditions many had come to hear him. After
the meeting was over he stayed behind to pray for people to be
filled with the Holy Spirit. After a short instruction talk and
prayer, Mr. Bennett moved slowly down a row of people, each
waiting reverently to receive the laying on of hands. When he
laid hands on a young girl's head, she began to speak confidently
in an unknown language. It sounded beautiful and filled the
room with a sense of awe; some had tears in their eyes as they
heard this girl "Rejoicing in the Holy Spirit." When Dennis
Bennett moved on to a minister and laid his hands on his head,
the reaction was the opposite to that of the young girl. He began
to growl like a dog and to flail his arms in all directions. He

3

slipped from his chair and went into a coma. The atmosphere changed dramatically. One realised that one was face to face with another power that had been exposed by the Holy Spirit and made to demonstrate its presence.

While Mr. Bennett continued his laying on of hands, the minister was taken to the main hall, where there were still a few people talking, while others were stacking the chairs away. The situation was explained, and the minister agreed that it was necessary to expel these evil powers. But the moment the name of Jesus was mentioned, he went into another coma, his legs shot from under him, and he lay spread-eagled and inert on the floor. Bending over him and binding the enemy power, the spirits were commanded to leave in the name of Jesus. He opened his eyes, blinked, got to his feet, brushed himself down and smiled blandly. He had been delivered.

That a minister should be able to go through his training and ordination and serve for several years in churches without anyone apparently knowing that he was in such serious bondage may be a little incredible, but not if we bear in mind that Jesus cast an evil spirit for the first time from a man in a synagogue. Presumably he had been attending that place of worship without much difficulty for a number of years.

This incident is an illustration of what this book is about. That behind the facade of religious life there is a spiritual battle raging. There seem to be many who are not fully aware of this warfare. From time to time there is a dramatic collision between the power of the Spirit and that of Satan. In that meeting that night Satan's grip on a young minister was first exposed and then loosed by the power of God. The battle will often not be as sharply defined as this; but it is no less real, and success for the Christian will depend in a large measure on recognising the work of the devil and knowing how to defeat and expel him from every situation.

Let it be emphasised that this book is concerned with spiritual warfare in general, not with discerning and expelling evil spirits in particular, which is one part of the total conflict. Confusion here has led some into a false and exaggerated emphasis on detecting evil spirits. More about this in a moment. Nevertheless, most Christians need to come face to face with the fact and significance of evil spirits and their activity in the world and the Church. Merrill F. Unger writes about this:

> Without such basic knowledge (demonology) the student of religions, no matter what his qualifications for his task may otherwise be, cannot be expected to make accurate evaluations or reach valid conclusions. His estimate both of Christianity and of non-Christian religions must be expected to be faulty and misleading.

The present world situation calls for a serious study of this subject. We are living at a time of expanding supernaturalism, good and bad. On the one hand there is the charismatic revival, already mentioned, which is seeking to allow the Holy Spirit freedom to manifest the power of God in the Church and in the world. But on the other hand, there is a resurgence of the power of evil supernaturalism on a truly daunting scale. This book is written to alert people to this spiritual warfare and the dangers of ignoring it.

Paul writes prophetically in 2 Timothy 3:1—"in the last days there will come times of stress." It is a most interesting word that Paul uses here—*chalepos*. It is only used twice in the New Testament, here and in Matthew 8:28, when it is used to describe the two demoniacs, who were so "fierce" that "none could pass that way." Souter translates this word "difficult to restrain"—suggesting a tremendous super-human and uncontrollable strength. Taylor in his modern translation graphically paraphrases the verse, "in the last days it is going to be very difficult to be a Christian." And so it is today! There is fierce conflict, and there are those who do not want to "pass this way." But we cannot avoid the battle—for if we do not fight the enemy, he will still come at us. This book is intended to expose the enemy in all his venom and cleverness, and to enable Christians to handle the weapons of God successfully and overcome him.

If we read on in the 2 Timothy 3 passage we see how aptly Paul seems to be describing our own days:

> For men will be lovers of self, lovers of money, proud, arrogant, abusive, disobedient to their parents, ungrateful, unholy, inhuman, implacable, slanderers, profligates, fierce, haters of good, treacherous, reckless, swollen with conceit, lovers of pleasure rather than lovers of God, holding the form of religion but denying the power of it.

Then in verse 8 Paul likens some of those people who have a "corrupt mind and counterfeit faith" to Jannes and Jambres, two of the magicians of Egypt who opposed Moses and counterfeited the miracles which he performed in the power of God. There are some today who lay claim to great powers, including the power to heal the sick, whose faith is "counterfeit."

I had hesitations about writing this book. For one thing, Satan does not like being exposed. He works secretly, and his success depends to a large extent on escaping detection. When one lays bare some of his strategems, one invites retaliation. Satan does not make life exactly easy—and writing a book like this will not improve the treatment. But that is a risk worth taking. After all Satan pays us compliments when he gives us special attention. My main hesitation has been over how some Christians will handle a book like this. There are, alas, good grounds for apprehension on this score. Harm has been caused by those who seem to see Satan at work in every situation. There have been some crude excesses in this area. Some have been known to have a so-called "deliverance ministry" which has brought confusion to some and led others in defence to close the door to the real as well as the counterfeit.

One fears those who will turn this book into a system to be applied in every instance. They will begin to see evil spirits in every situation and may begin to minister without the real equipment to sustain such exacting ministry. One fears for those who may be caused to stumble by their behaviour. Extremists have been known to take advantage of the ignorance of Christians on this subject. Demonic agency has been attributed to every personal and public ill. If funds are not available, it is blamed on demons. Heresy (especially the expression of teaching not held by themselves) is said to be of demonic origin. Sins of the flesh are due to demonic possession. If people are thought to be "churchy," then the fault lies in "religious demons!" These bizarre diagnostics have one infallible and inevitable cure for all ills—the casting out of demons. Of course occasionally, by coincidence, they are right. And this only spurs them on to further ministry. When there is failure, little attempt is made to accept the blame themselves. The fruit unfortunately is often bitter not sweet, and it all seems a far cry from the sane and balanced treatment of the subject in the New Testament.

But in spite of this the book had to be written. We urgently need to understand more clearly the nature of spiritual warfare in all its complexity, as well as knowing how to deal with evil spirits when they are detected. One might equally ignore Paul's epistles and their doctrines, or even the scriptures altogether, because even in the days of the apostle Peter there were things in them which "the ignorant and unstable twist to their own destruction" (2 Peter 3:16). This book is not recommended as suitable reading matter for the "unstable."

This is a somewhat dangerous subject, but unavoidable if one is really concerned about the renewal of the Church. For many years the Church's defences have been down, and the enemy has made deep incursions into it. The Holy Spirit comes to reveal the enemy and expose him to the powerful attacks of God's people. In the synagogue that morning, the evil spirit was forced to cry out because a truly Spirit-filled teacher, the Son of God, was there.

And it is not a nice or neat subject. It will be unpalatable to any whose idea of the Church is something cosy and orderly. The man in the synagogue upset the liturgy that morning. To see people demonstrating in this way may be degrading. The Gadarene demoniac was not exactly a tourist attraction; in fact, people avoided the place where he lived among the tombs. But Jesus visited him, with remarkable and permanent results. We should not shirk this matter simply because it is unpleasant. It may upset the decorum of humdrum church life. But it may be that this kind of decorum is not worth preserving. It could be an anaesthetic to save us from facing up to the realities of spiritual warfare. In shutting our minds to those possibilities we may be shutting out God the Holy Spirit. God does want to demonstrate his ability to conquer these powers, and they often need to be activated before they can be dealt with. Why should we think of our churches as convalescent homes for people to "recover" while insulated from the pressures of the outside world, instead of hospitals where often radical and sometimes painful surgery is the only answer to deep needs?

There are three pathways to avoid. The first is that of denying the existence of evil spirits and Satan, and taking an unrealistic and benevolent view of the world and man in it. The second is to attribute all spiritual experience to God, including forbidden territory. This is a road that leads to destruction. The third is that of attributing most, sometimes even all, evil and sin to Satan and demonic activity. This is the error of dualism, and we shall be elaborating this later.

Each of these pathways takes the easy way out. They avoid the necessity for "discernment." In the Greek this word (*diakrisis*) is the word from which we get the English word "crisis." It implies the making of a decision, distinguishing between right and wrong, and, therefore, inevitably arriving at some judgement. We naturally shrink from this. We would rather lump everything together and stick one label on it.

The answer does not lie in closing our eyes to the whole subject, but having them opened wider so that we can see what is truly of God, what is human and what is satanic. It is a hard road to travel, and calls for constant vigilance and a closeness to our Lord which is sacrificial, disciplined, at times dangerous, and unpopular with some. It is this pathway that we are proposing in this book. It is not intended as a case book, although some cases are cited, nor as a comprehensive textbook. But we trust it points people in the right direction, and gives them a balanced and sane approach to a difficult but important subject.

TWO

The Day Star Falls

THE BIBLE SAYS very little about the origin of evil. The writers are only permitted a brief glimpse now and then into the mystery of the fall of Satan. Isaiah tells how the "day star," as Satan is called, fell from grace through pride:

> How you are fallen from heaven,
>   O Day Star, son of Dawn!
> How you are cut down to the ground,
>   you who laid the nations low!
> You said in your heart,
>   "I will ascend to heaven;
> Above the stars of God
>   I will set my throne on high;
> I will sit on the mount of assembly
>   in the far north;
> I will ascend above the heights of the clouds,
>   I will make myself like the Most High."
>   (Isaiah 14:12-14)

The other reference is even more oblique. It comes in Ezekiel:

> Moreover the word of the Lord came to me:
> "Son of man,
>   raise a lamentation over the king of Tyre,
>   and say to him,
>   Thus says the Lord GOD:

9

"You were the signet of perfection,
   full of wisdom
   and perfect in beauty.
You were in Eden, the garden of God;
   every precious stone was your covering,
   carnelian, topaz, and jasper,
   chrysolite, beryl, and onyx,
sapphire, carbuncle, and emerald;
   and wrought in gold were your settings
   and your engravings.
On the day you were created
   they were prepared.
With an anointed guardian cherub I placed you;
   you were on the holy mountain of God;
   in the midst of the stones of fire you walked.
You were blameless in your ways
   from the days you were created,
   till iniquity was found in you.
In the abundance of your trade
   you were filled with violence, and you sinned;
so I cast you as a profane thing from the mountain of God,
   and the guardian cherub drove you out
   from the midst of the stones of fire.
Your heart was proud because of your beauty;
   you corrupted your wisdom for the sake of your splendour.
I cast you to the ground;
   I exposed you before kings,
   to feast their eyes on you.
By the multitude of your iniquities,
   in the unrighteousness of your trade
   you profaned your sanctuaries;
so I brought forth fire from the midst of you;
   it consumed you,
and I turned you to ashes upon the earth
   in the sight of all who saw you.

                        (Ezek. 28:11-18)

In both these passages we see that the fall of Satan is attributed to pride and vanity. And Satan is not an ugly monster with horns, but "perfect in beauty" in his original state. No wonder he is able to masquerade as an angel of light!

There is not much written about Satan or his agents, the demons, in the Old Testament. We have to wait for the Light of the world to appear before the darkness is fully exposed. The early history of the people of God describes, on the whole, a separated nomadic race, having little or no contact with the pagan world around it, until it became incarcerated in Egypt. But their aspirations for freedom and their hatred of the Egyptians meant they were reasonably free from the paganising influences of the Egyptians and their religions.

But the battle really began when they were expatriated from Egypt and brought into the Promised Land. When they entered Canaan they came face to face for the first time with advanced forms of spiritual wickedness. The Jews rightly labelled these rival religions "demonic." Moses knew that they were sacrificing to demons "which were no gods" (Deut. 32:17)—even at times their sons and daughters (Ps. 106:37). There is no doubt that these pagan cults had a strongly occultic and spiritualistic flavour. Sexual orgies, human sacrifices, powers of foretelling the future and revealing secrets, calling up the dead and other forms of mediumistic activity featured in these rites. The Jews were correct—they did have a demonic basis. This is one explanation for the ruthless genocide ordered by the army of occupation. These people were novices at spiritual warfare, and they were living on the other side of the decisiveness of Christ's victory over these powers at Calvary. In coming into contact with these awesome powers, the only remedy *then* was to destroy them root and branch. When this was not done, then they themselves were very likely to succumb.

The attitude of the heathen world to these things is epitomised by the interesting fact that the word "demon" (*daimon*) in classical Greek (or the diminutive *daimonion*) was frequently used in a good sense, even to describe a god, or one with divine power. It was sometimes used interchangeably with *theos*, meaning "god." So we see there was little concern for discrimination between good and evil.

The Promised Land before its occupation by the armies of Israel was riddled with all kinds of evil supernaturalism. There is a list given of them in Deuteronomy 18:10-11—human sacrifices, divination, soothsaying, augury, sorcery, and various forms of spiritualism, normally referred to as necromancy. Many a hill and mountain was marked and scarred with the remains of disgusting heathen idolatry. Those who indulged in these things were "an abomination to the Lord" (Deut. 18:12), and because of these practises God was "driving them out" before them. God did not allow them to do these things, but He promised to give them a prophet like Moses (Deut. 18:15). God would put his words into Moses' mouth, and this was the divinely ordained way for his people to hear his voice and know his will, and thus all dangers and pitfalls would be avoided.

The word "divination" is a general term which covers all attempts to obtain information from the spiritual world other than through the word of God, the revelation of the Holy Spirit, or any other divinely appointed channels. Divination has always been forbidden the children of God, and this absolute prohibition has never been rescinded.

One of the main forms of divination is "necromancy." This is a word derived from two Greek words—*manteia*, meaning "soothsaying," and *nekros*, meaning "the dead." In other words it means communicating with the dead, or what is called today spiritualism (or spiritism). The person who practises this is called in the Bible a wizard or a medium. The "go-between" is called "a familiar spirit." This is the Authorised Version translation, and is derived from the thought of a close family servant. But the Hebrew word literally means "hollow" and is thought to apply either to the caves in which the mediums sought to contact the dead, or to the sound the "spirit" made when it spoke through the lips of the medium.

The Old Testament is adamant about this whole area. It is forbidden territory, and those who trespass into it do so at their peril. It cost King Saul his life in battle, for in 1 Chronicles 10:13 we are told he "died for his unfaithfulness; he was unfaithful to the Lord in that he did not keep the command of the Lord, and also consulted a medium, seeking guidance, and did not seek guidance from the Lord. Therefore the Lord slew him, and turned the kingdom over to David the son of Jesse." The Mosaic law is categorical in its prohibitions. "Do not turn to mediums or wizards; do not seek them out, to be defiled by them: I am the Lord your God" (Lev. 19:31). Or again, "if a person turns to mediums and wizards, playing the harlot after them, I will set my face against that person, and will cut him off from among his people" (Lev. 20:6). Mediums and wizards were to be put to death by stoning (Lev. 20:27). The same penalty was to be applied to those practising sorcery (Exod. 22:18). Samuel equated divination with disobedience and called it categorically a sin (1 Sam. 15:23).

The kings to a very large extent prospered or failed as they either condemned or condoned this evil. Manasseh provoked God to anger when he involved himself in all these practises (2 Chron. 33:6). Josiah, on the other hand, "put away the mediums and the wizards" when he turned to the Lord with all his heart (2 Kings 23:24).

The Bible condemns all forms of spiritualism. It is wrong in itself. But it is as much an act of unfaithfulness as it is of disobedience. It implies that God has not provided adequate channels and the means of hearing his voice and discovering his will. Isaiah challenged the people of his day who had been resorting to spiritualism: "and when they say to you 'Consult the mediums and the wizards who chirp and mutter,' should not a people consult their God? Should they consult the dead on behalf of the living? To the teaching and to the testimony! Surely for this word which they speak there is no dawn" (Isa. 8:19-20). To consult mediums and make contact with the dead is to break faith with God.

There is a very clear example of this in the Old Testament. In 1 Samuel 28 we find King Saul needing guidance before a battle. He could not turn to Samuel, for the prophet was dead.

When he consulted God there was no answer, due to the king's disobedience. So in his frustration and indecision he resorted to a spiritist medium. This was not so easy, as the king had banished them all from the land. So he asked one of his servants to find him one. And so we read of the clandestine visit of the disguised king in the dead of night to the medium at Endor. The king asked for contact with the deceased prophet Samuel, but neither he nor the medium bargained for the personal appearance of the prophet which was to follow.

One thing is clear from this account: the woman was used to dealing fraudulently with her customers. She got the shock of her life when the real prophet appeared! This is not an example of the normal procedure whereby people contact the spirit of a dead person. This was a unique reappearance of a dead man, not for the purpose of blessing or comfort, but to rebuke the king and pronounce judgement upon him. And as we have already seen, Saul paid for this final act of disobedience with his life on the field of battle the very next day. And times have not changed, for those who practise spiritualism, or dabble in it, trespass into territory which God has declared "out of bounds" to all. They risk serious harm to their souls and bodies.

But it is not only necromancy that is forbidden the people of God; all other forms of divination are likewise. In the heathen world at that time, and for centuries to follow, all kinds of strange practises were followed to secure guidance or success in battle, procreation or the fertility of crops. There was belomancy (shooting arrows), astrology (consulting the stars), hepatoscopy (examining the liver of animals). All of these, and every other form of divination, are forbidden the people of God. The king of Babylon might use such methods (see Ezek. 21:21), but not the Israelites. These practises are all included in such terms as "sorcery" or "augury," and listed as forbidden in Leviticus together with necromancy.

The practise of wearing charms as protection was common in the ancient world, and no doubt this form of superstition spilled over into Israel as faith diminished. In Isaiah 3 we find listed with "the mighty man," the soldier, the judge and the prophet—"the diviner," "the skilful magician" and the "expert in charms." No wonder the prophet pronounces judgement upon them in no uncertain terms. Later in the same chapter he denounces the fashionable women not only for wearing expensive jewelry, but for wearing "crescents" (3:18), which were charms worn around the neck as protection against evil.

Merrill F. Unger suggests that this may have been the reason why the Pharisees wore their phylacteries—they had a magical connotation.[2] The practise was a corruption of the commandment of Exodus 13:9, 16. The Greek word itself means to guard or to protect. By the time of Jesus the law had taken on a quasi-magical character. It could be used as a lucky talisman and be worn for protection.

But, as we shall see later, we have much of this superstition still with us. Today the fate of football matches is supposed to hinge on which boot is put on first. The carrying of mascots, the wearing of amulets and St. Christopher medals, is very common, even among Christians. Faith in such forms of protection is forbidden the people of God, for He has provided really effective ways of keeping us safe, and we shall be considering these later in the book. To trust in these other things implies lack of faith and confidence in God himself.

Thus we see in the Old Testament that there are very clear lines of demarcation between the real and the counterfeit. Penalties are sterner in this field than almost any other. Both spiritualism and adultery are punishable by death. God knew that the invasion of spiritualism and the breakdown of morals were two of the greatest dangers facing Israel. The full impact of this has in one way been lost by the translators of the Authorised Version using the words "witch" or "witchcraft" to describe what should really be translated "sorcery." "Witch" is a loaded word. It means literally "one who knows"—or in other words "a diviner"—but it conjures up pictures of the hags in *Macbeth*, stirring up their pot, or the equally malevolent creation of Walt Disney in "Snow White and the Seven Dwarfs," who has frightened succeeding generations of children. Such witches originated probably in the rather overactive imagination of those living in medieval times. The Bible is not primarily thinking of such people, whether they ever really existed or not. It is referring to people, of whom there are far too many today, who imagine they can break God's laws with impunity and bypass the means of communication clearly laid down by God. Both in the Old and New Covenants He has made it abundantly clear how He is to be approached, how his voice is to be heard, and how his will is to be known. The days of witchcraft or sorcery are not by any means over. In fact there is a revival of it throughout Europe. But we are not to think in terms of old women on broomsticks, but rather something more sophisticated and, therefore, more deadly. We must now turn to discovering the remedy for the power of Satan and how God's Son came to triumph over these forces.

THREE

Far Above All

Posterity shall serve him; men shall tell of the Lord to the coming generation, and proclaim his deliverance to a people yet unborn, that he has wrought it (that it, is finished, [Amplified]).   Ps. 22:30-31

WITH THE COMING OF JESUS CHRIST we see the perfect demonstration of what this book is all about. For He exposed the enemy and drew him into open conflict. Then he defeated him utterly and completely. The twilight of the pre-Christian era gave way suddenly and dramatically to the noonday sun of the glory of Christ.

Jesus was under assault throughout his earthly life. He was a marked man. The enemy constantly tried to destroy Him or divert Him from his divinely appointed pathway of life. The moment He was born a determined attempt was made on his life, and only the intervention of an angel and a hurried journey into Egypt saved the young child from death. During his public ministry there were several sinister plots and at least one attempt at assassination, which proved abortive. His encounter with Satan in the wilderness, at the start of his ministry, was only the prelude to many other attacks. In the end they came through his own disciples—first Peter, who tried to prevent Him from accepting the road to Calvary, and then Judas, whom Satan finally entered and used to betray his own master.

17

But the initiative was not always Satan's. For wherever Jesus went He upset and overthrew his kingdom. He healed those who were oppressed by him (Acts 10:38), loosed a woman who had been bound by him for eighteen years (Luke 13:16), and on numerous occasions delivered those whose personalities had been invaded by his evil spirits.

This was all part of the purpose of his coming. Jesus himself declared, "He has sent me to proclaim release to the captives . . . to set at liberty those who are oppressed" (Luke 4:18). So He fulfilled the prophecy of Isaiah. A new day had dawned, "to give light to those who sit in darkness and in the shadow of death," as Zechariah described it (Luke 1:79). But when this light shone into the darkness there were often sharp reactions. "Do not torment me," shouted the demoniac at Jesus (Mark 5:17). For a being that habitually lives in darkness, the coming of light can be torture, not blessing. And this is what the coming of Jesus to this earth meant. As Merrill F. Unger has described it:

> It was the unavoidable collision of the unhindered power of the Holy Spirit manifested through a sinless life with the opposing power of Satan. It was impossible for the Son of God to be in the vicinity of evil power, and not expose it and challenge it. Shadows of twilight and the curtain of night only temporarily hide what the brilliance of the noonday sun reveals.

But a new and important stage had been reached in the age-long battle against the powers of darkness. Before Christ came, the light was to be preserved within the boundaries of God's chosen people, the Jews. But Christ proclaimed its future effusion throughout the world. So Simeon prophesied of this salvation, that it was "a light for revelation to the Gentiles" (Luke 2:32). The Church was to take the gospel to every nation, and to those who were in a special way under "the commander of the spiritual powers of the air," the spirit then at work "among God's rebel subjects" (Eph. 2:2 NEB). No longer were the people of God to live a life of national separation. They were to move out into all the world, and so they were to need in a new way power to deal with the spiritual wickedness that they were going to encounter. So Paul conceived his mission to the Gentiles in terms of turning them "from darkness to light and from the power of Satan to God" (Acts 26:18). The apostle John looked out on a world, the whole of which was "in the power of the evil one" (1 John 5:19).

But before this mission could begin, the enemy had to be defeated and disarmed. Jesus achieved this on the Cross. It is most important to see the dual purpose of that death. It is summarised perfectly for us by John in his first epistle—"he appeared to take away sins . . . the reason the Son of God appeared was to destroy [literally 'undo'] the works of the devil" (1 John 3:5 and 8). At the Cross man's sin was cleansed and Satan's power broken. To use some of the imagery of Charles Wesley's hymns—sinners lost both their guilty stains and their heavy chains. Satan's strong grip on the world was slackened, and the way was opened for the Church, in the power and authority of the Spirit, to deliver millions of prisoners Satan had in chains throughout the world.

Paul put both aspects of the Cross very graphically when he wrote to the Colossians how Christ had "cancelled the bond which stood against us with its legal demands; this he set aside, nailing it to the cross." He dealt thoroughly with our sins and our just condemnation. But we need to read on. "He disarmed the principalities and powers and made a public example of them, triumphing over them in it" (or "him," which is an alternative reading) (Col. 2:14-15). As Ronald Knox puts it in his translation—He robbed the dominion and powers of their prey. The same truth is expressed clearly by Paul in his address in the synagogue at Antioch of Pisidia (Acts 13:38-39). Through Jesus there is not only forgiveness of sins but freedom from everything "from which you could not be freed by the law of Moses."

But in Ephesians Paul takes the triumph a stage further from the Cross by linking it also with the resurrection and the ascension of our Lord, and expressing what these events mean in terms of victory over Satan. Speaking of Christ's new position, he writes of it as "far above all rule and authority and power and dominion, and above every name that is named, not only in this age but also in that which is to come; and he has put all things under his feet and has made him the head over all things for the church, which is his body, the fulness of him who fills all in all" (Eph. 1:21-23). And in quoting from Psalm 68:18 he refers again to Christ being far all, after he had "led captivity captive" (A.V.).

And He is still there —far above all! What confidence this should give us in our warfare against Satan! Now the Church can penetrate the dark jungles of the world, protected from danger and able to tame them in the power of Jesus' name.

Here we are dealing with the bed-rock of any successful ministry in the field of spiritual warfare. We dare not enter into battle without a firm confidence in the efficacy of the death of Christ and a firm trust in the power of his new position in the heavenlies.

As we read the gospels we not only come into a new realisation of the reality of Christ's victory, but also a new understanding of the nature of those malevolent forces working under their supreme commander. Not only is Satan exposed by the light of Christ's coming, but so also are the evil spirits, of which we read so little in the Old Testament. Here we are able to learn very much more about their nature and mode of operation.

We know from the New Testament that these spirits are not the souls of dead people. They are rather fallen angels, who were evicted from heaven at the same time as their commander, Satan. In Revelation 12:7 there is a reference to Satan *and his angels* fighting with Michael and his, and Satan is thrown down to the earth with his angels. In Matthew 25:41 Jesus uses the same description in referring to "the devil and his angels." In Jude 6 and 2 Peter 2:4 there is a reference to fallen angels and their fate. It seems clear too that in Romans 8:38 the angels referred to are not God's angels but Satan's, for God's would hardly be described as separating us from the love of God in Christ Jesus our Lord. It may also be true that in the rather obscure text which refers to women wearing veils "because of the angels" (1 Cor. 11:10), it refers to Satan's angels, not God's.

These evil spirits are personalities, like God's angels, not impersonal influences. They are agents working under the authority of Satan. They can speak (Mark 5:9, 12), believe (James 2:19), exercise their wills (Luke 11:24), and they know about their future fate (Matt. 8:29) and recognise Jesus as the Son of God (Mark 1:24), and so clearly possess intelligence. But, like Satan, they ultimately only operate within the permissive will of God, and on occasions they fulfil his will (see, for example, Psalm 78:49).

Sometimes these beings are called demons in the New Testament, the usual Greek word being *daimonion,* the diminutive of *daimon.* But in six places they are called "evil spirits" (*ponera*), and in twenty-three, *"unclean spirits" (akatharta).* They desire to possess living organisms—human beings, but also animals. In the gospels, for instance, we are told how they entered into pigs (Mark 5:13). They sometimes exert a physical influence on people either enduing them with superhuman strength, as in the case of the demoniac who "broke his fetters in pieces" (Mark 5:4), or affecting one or more of their organs. In a later chapter we shall be analysing the various areas of satanic attack and giving examples of how these attacks can be recognised and dealt with accordingly.

We see Jesus completely in command of the situation when faced with satanic power. "Begone, Satan!" He tells him in the wilderness; "Get behind me, Satan!" He says to Peter. He silenced and rebuked the evil spirits, and cast them out with a word. They came cringing to Him when they had been cast out of the demoniac, begging Him to let them go into the pigs. Only when permission was given were they able to enter in. Throughout the gospels Jesus reveals his complete authority and mastery over these unseen forces of evil.

The life of Jesus is our perfect example of how to conduct spiritual warfare. Before his coming, the law had only one answer to entrenched evil—the death penalty. But from Pentecost onwards the Church was able to wield a new weapon—the all victorious name of Jesus and the power of the Holy Spirit. So what Jesus had so successfully accomplished throughout the brief period of his earthly ministry was to be enacted many times over in the years to come. Because Jesus had gone to the Father and released the full power of the Holy Spirit, Christians are able to do even greater works. The success and failure of the Church in this matter is the subject of the next chapter.

FOUR

The Triumphal Procession

*But thanks be to God, who continually leads us about,
captives in Christ's triumphal procession, and everywhere
uses us to reveal and spread abroad the fragrance of the
knowledge of himself.*   2 Cor. 2:14 NEB

PAUL LIKENED HIMSELF and his Christian brothers to "captives
in Christ's triumphal procession." To men of all generations
such "victory parades" have had their appeal. In Paul's day
there were the great occasions when Roman generals returned
from their successes on the battlefield, dragging behind them
their prisoners—the evidence for all to see of the great triumph
which had been secured. In our day we see the same enthusiasm when astronauts return from space, bringing back with
them their photographs or specimens of lunar rocks, or
football teams when they return to their home cities after
victory in a Cup final. So Paul sees Christ's great triumphal
procession in this light—and what a trophy of that triumph he
himself was! Day by day, he saw more captives added—
cumulative evidence of Christ's victory over all his enemies.

That is what the whole of church history down to the present
day should have been like. At times the ranks of the procession
have been swollen with captives. But at other times they have
thinned and almost faded away. But it all began with high
hopes.

From the start the battle was fierce. On the one hand there

was the opposition of the Jews. The Christians were persecuted, forbidden to preach or teach, beaten, imprisoned, maligned and vilified, excommunicated and put to death. But Jesus had warned them that this would happen. Satan also was actively at work behind the scenes—no doubt encouraging the persecution itself, but also working as a fifth column within the Church. It was ominous for the future that the first direct mention of his activity was within the fellowship. Soon after Pentecost he had succeeded in infiltrating the body of Christ. The occasion was the deceit of a married couple named Ananias and Sapphira, who made out that they had given everything to the Church, but had secretly held back something for themselves. The Holy Spirit exposed their deceit. Peter was given the information that was necessary to bring this hypocrisy into the open—"why has Satan filled your heart to lie to the Holy Spirit?" he asked the husband. Both died when they realised that their sin had been discovered. There was subtraction as well as addition in the Church in those days.

But the signal for full scale spiritual warfare came when the Church emerged from its Jewish environment in Jerusalem and began to move out into Samaria and the rest of the world. The Spirit-filled Church immediately came into conflict with satanic powers. Again and again there are clashes between the gospel and occultism and other spiritual forces. The triumphal procession grew as allegiances switched from Satan to God.

The first occasion arose when the boundaries of the Christian community were suddenly extended beyond Jerusalem because of a great persecution in the city itself. The Church was scattered, but so was the gospel! A man named Philip went to a Samaritan city and began to minister there. He not only preached to them, but cast unclean spirits out of many and healed large numbers who were lame or paralysed. This, as usual, drew a large crowd and commanded their attention. They accepted his message and were baptised. One of the onlookers was a man called Simon, who had been working for the enemy. He too had collected a large following, and for a long time had amazed them with his magical powers. He had told them that he was some great personage, perhaps the re-incarnation of some dead dignitary. But even this man had to recognise that a greater power was at work, and it is surely no coincidence that it was in the area where the evil man had been ministering that Philip found so many people in need of deliverance from unclean spirits. Wherever necromancy and sorcery are to be found, we may expect similar needs.

Then in Acts 13 we have the record of the first commissioning of evangelists to take the gospel into the heart of heathenism. Almost at once we discover them confronted with satanic power. It came this time from another magician—Bar-Jesus, a Jewish false prophet, who tried to prevent Sergius Paulus, an intelligent Roman official, from hearing the word of God. Paul does not mince words with this godless heckler. He calls him "a son of the devil" and "an enemy of all righteousness." Paul predicts that blindness will come temporarily upon him. No wonder the proconsul believed when he saw what happened! Again it was obvious for everyone to see that God's power was greater than the power of Satan, and that the Church had the authority to deal with people who interfered with the preaching of the word of God.

Later in Philippi (Acts 16), with his new partner Silas, Paul is in the centre of another clash between the Holy Spirit and Satan. This time it is a girl with a so-called "python" spirit. Luke deliberately uses the verb *manteuomai*, which had pagan associations, to describe her activity. The word *"python"* literally means a ventriloquist, as the person possessed spoke with their lips closed like modern ventriloquists do; and the word is derived from the name of a town called Pytho near Mt. Parnassus, where the mythological serpent was supposed to live. However, the evil spirit is cast out, and a riot follows. Paul and Silas receive a beating in public and an evening in prison. God dramatically intervenes, releasing the prisoners and converting the jailer. It is dangerously exciting when Satan's hornet nests are stirred up.

In Acts 19 there is another invasion of enemy territory. This time it is Ephesus, an area of strong satanic influence. Here the sons of Sceva were doing their best to imitate Paul. But when the break-through came there was a huge bon-fire made of the magical books and other relics of satanic practices. There was a public confession of these evil procedures. But so many had been contaminated and needed deliverance that our Lord had to use the extraordinary method of Paul's handkerchiefs and aprons to bring them into freedom.

The heathen world of that time was shot through and through with superstitious practices which had to be confessed and renounced when people surrendered their lives to Christ. Pagan sacrifices were offered to demons, so Paul tells us (1 Cor. 10:20), and Christians were to have nothing to do with them.

As the gospel spread into the pagan areas of the world, this conflict continued. No compromise was permitted. The attitude of Christian leaders was as obdurate as that of Moses and Joshua in the Old Testament. Very early on there came into normal Christian initiation the rite of exorcism, which indicates that many of the early pagan converts must have been contaminated by demonic powers. There was very little atheism or agnosticism in those days, and many gave their all to dark and dangerous doctrines. This exorcism rite has remained to this day in the Roman Catholic service of baptism. "It has always been applied to catechumens (baptismal candidates)," says the *Oxford Dictionary of the Christian Church*.[4] This concept also strongly flavours the Orthodox rite of baptism, for the service is thought of as a dramatic snatching of a child from the clutches of Satan into the hands of Christ. In the Church of England rite of baptism, exorcism appeared in the first of Cranmer's Prayer Books (1549), but disappeared afterwards in the wave of reactionary feeling which wanted to see the Prayer Book stripped of all so-called superstitious connotations.

As pagan life and culture were penetrated by the Church, there was a relentless attempt to rid the face of the earth of all vestige of satanic power. Churches were actually built on the sites of pagan shrines to make sure they would never again be used for evil practices. The date of Christmas was deliberately chosen to coincide with a pagan festival. The missionaries in those early centuries were charismatically inspired. They would never have survived the rigours of their calling had they not possessed sensitivity to the Holy Spirit as well as to the powers of darkness, and a strong faith in the name of Jesus. We are inclined in a more scientific age to scoff at them and ascribe their actions to ignorance. But maybe they were the realists and we the blind leaders of the blind.

But gradually the procession dwindles. The Church becomes highly organised, the surest way of quenching the Spirit. The missionary zeal of the early centuries lost its impetus. The Church, which was supposed to have conquered the Roman Empire, is itself conquered by the spirit of Rome—authoritarian and legalistic. The bureaucrats and ecclesiastical politicians take over. Now we see superstition taking the place of true discernment. We find the Church becoming corrupt and paganised. It encourages superstition and is quite unable to cope with the widespread outbreaks of demonic activity and rampant witchcraft. At the same time we notice, as one would expect, that the sharp distinctions between the powers of God and of Satan become bleared, and the Church seems unable to distinguish between the gifts of the Holy Spirit and the manifestations of demons. It is interesting to notice that the supposed symptoms of demon-possession and witchcraft out-lined in the *Rituale Romanum*, which was the standard textbook on exorcism in the Middle Ages in the Western Church, include powers that aptly describe some of the gifts of the Holy Spirit. Indeed most of the gifts of the Spirit, outlined by Paul in 1 Corinthians 12, are included!

The Reformation changed most of this. It was one part of a vast movement which had its roots in the "new philosophy" of Thomas Aquinas, who enthroned reason over all else. The intellect, he taught, was the one part of man that was not involved in the Fall. The new thinking of this period marked the death-knell of superstition. But it threw the baby out with the bath-water, for the charismatic element went too. In the birth period of scientific enlightenment in the seventeenth century, through the work of men like Galileo, Descartes, Isaac Newton and others, the crudities of medieval superstition largely disappeared. It was the beginning of the age of reason. The Reformers and Puritans poured scorn on practices like the veneration of images and relics, healing shrines, holy places, and so on. Anything that could not pass the test of reason was probably diabolical.

But although the age of reason called in question the whole basis of demonic activity, it did not eliminate it. Moreover the eighteenth century marked the beginning of a new phase of missionary expansion which brought the Church into conflict once more with entrenched evil. The distinguished Church historian, the late K.S. Latourette, refers to many conversions in China which brought relief also in terms of demon possession. And this type of experience was common in many other parts of the world where Christian missions were working. The procession was really on the move again.

This is only a very sketchy account of many centuries of history. But we live again in a revolutionary century, when every previous way of thought is being called into question. The dominance of reason is being overthrown. For more than a century the doors have been wide open for a new reign of satanic power. But at the same time God is equipping his people to respond fully to these attacks.

FIVE

The Devil's Pentecost

The devil is shamming dead, but he is never busier than now.
Charles Kingsley

IN THE AUTUMN OF 1963 a man was released from an evil spell that had bound him for eleven years. He confessed to a minister that he had been baptised as a Satanist in May 1950. On being received into membership he was given the devil's mark—a tiny, star-shaped tattoo on the right forearm. According to this man witchcraft was being practised openly by businessmen, civil servants and artists. About this matter he said, "The less said about these ceremonies the better, because there is something inexplicable about witchcraft when properly practised. There is some unknown force or power which does work for evil."

About this time the Convocations of Canterbury and York were debating the new catechism. In a discussion this "parliament" of the Church of England just squeezed the devil in at the last minute. Some were questioning whether he really existed at all.

Charles Kingsley's words apply today. Satan is still shamming dead, and still on active service. In 1967 my wife and I were staying with an Anglican Vicar in New Zealand. My eyes caught the caption of an article in a magazine—"the devil's Pentecost." Picking it up I discovered that it was about a new and powerful movement in Japan called Soka Gakkai. The article described the fanatical zeal of the members of this new religion, and its incredible success. It then boasted a daily newspaper with a 3-million circulation. They had begun work on a temple, which when complete would be the largest religious building in the world, greater even than St. Peter's, Rome. They had embarked on a programme of world outreach. Since 1960 they had trebled their membership to over 6 million families. Their creed? "You are important; develop your capacities." Certainly something to appeal to modern man! Soka Gakkai mocks every basic Christian belief.

The caption gives a clue to the success of this movement. We are living in days when Satan is pouring out his spirits as well as Jesus Christ the Holy Spirit. In the Revelation, the activities of evil spirits are foretold as part of the total conflict of the Church with the powers of darkness. In chapter 9 there is a terrifying vision of the shaft of the bottomless pit being opened to release "locusts" that swarm over the earth, deceiving and destroying. But most of the world does not repent, but continues to worship demons (verse 20). Later in the same book there is a vision of the dragon, the beast and the false prophet, and from each of their mouths there come "foul spirits like frogs, for they are demonic spirits, performing signs . . ." (16:13). Yet again, we discover that the other powerful agency of evil in the Revelation, Babylon, is under the same influence. We are told that this symbol of affluence "has become a dwelling place for demons, a haunt of every foul spirit . . ." (18:2).

As we draw nearer to Christ's return there is no indication of a lessening of this power. The idea that evil spirits only operate in "uncivilised" parts of the world is entirely illusory. It may be true that at some points in history the power of a Church which believed in both the existence of such evil powers and the authority it possessed in Christ's name to overcome them, had removed most of this power from its borders or driven it underground and so neutralised its effectiveness. But such a situation does not exist today, for the Church has largely abdicated its authority and blandly disbelieves in such things. The enemy has come in a like a flood, and few have resisted it. Merrill F. Unger has written:[5]

Although demonic activity in human history has always been undeniably great since the sin of our first parents exposed mankind to its baneful attacks, yet the full realization and augmentation of its destructive power are reserved for the consummation of the age. Demonism bears a striking relation to the doctrine of the last things; and all classes of mankind, Jew, Gentile and the Church of God (1 Cor. 10:32), will be intimately and vitally affected by the last-day upsurge of evil supernaturalism.

So let us look at some aspects of this hideous outpouring.

Witchcraft

We have already mentioned one example of this, but in recent years in many parts of the world there has been a return of witchcraft in all its ugliness and its many disgusting ceremonies, and it is attracting people from many walks of life. It has been popularised by writers such as Denis Wheatley. Barely a week goes by without references to it in the press, and TV and films have increased their quota of programmes on the subject.

In Britain this fascination for the occult is growing rapidly. One of the most popular games sold at Christmas 1968 was the Ouija board, an old form of magic whereby "messages" are received through the agency of spirits. In 1969 a school was opened in Essex for would-be witches. The organiser boasted, "I'm not ashamed of witchcraft, really we are quite normal." In March of the same year there was a report in the student paper of Aston University that the Psychical Research Society had been closed down when satanism infiltrated it. The report went on, "The evidence is mounting that more people are dabbling in these sinister activities, and over the last 18 months there have been several suicide attempts by people influenced by occult activities."[6] In the same report there was the heartening news that the same society had lost 50 per cent of its members, who had been converted in a student mission in the university. In San Francisco the First Satanic "Church" has been founded, and it is known that devil worship is actively practised throughout the world. Churches in this country are being broken into, and cemeteries invaded for black masses held in mockery of the Lord's Supper.

Divination

We have already seen how divination is condemned in the Old Testament, and the people of God are forbidden to use any forms of it. But this century has seen the widespread growth of many forms of divination, both for the purposes of foretelling the future and for diagnosing disease. When we visited New Zealand in 1967 we found various forms of divination being widely practised. At a meeting in Christchurch, when the sin of divination was clearly stated, a woman got to her feet and confessed that she had been to a chiropractor who had employed this method in his treatment of her various ailments, which had only partially been successful. When she made a full confession to God, hands were laid on her and the Lord Jesus Christ healed her fully.

In several parts of the world there is great deal of colour-therapy (chromotherapy) being practised. By means of divination (often through the use of a wooden rod) a diagnosis is made of the cause of the illness and the colours required for treatment. The patient is then subjected by various means of apparatus to these "healing rays." The history of this form of treatment, according to its teachers, goes back to the sun worship of Egypt and the teaching of Indian and Chinese mystics. There is no Christian basis for it whatsoever, and both its teaching and its methods are in direct opposition to the plain teaching of the word of God.

But colour-therapy is only one small part of the total resurgence of divination, which is sprouting up in many guises throughout the world. It gets results, otherwise no one would bother with it. But results are not everything—it is more important to be obedient to the revealed will of God, and then the results will take care of themselves. This increase is partly due to the increasing worldliness of the Church and its members, and partly to the drab materialism of the world, which between them are creating a huge vacuum, with millions of people hungry for spiritual experience and something to help them see beyond what they see with their eyes. Man has always wanted to explore the unknown, and many have an insatiable curiosity to know about the future. So more and more people are resorting to diviners of one kind or another—fortune-tellers, palm-readers, crystal-ball gazers, and the popular horoscopes which are part of the indispensable diet of millions of people in newspapers and magazines.

In the United States there are reputed to be over 5,000 people working full-time charting the heavens for over 10 million Americans who seek their services. The phenomenal success of America's Jeanne Dixon, who predicted amongst other things President Kennedy's assassination, can be gauged from the sales of her book *A Gift of Prophecy: the Phenomenal Jeanne Dixon.* The sales have exceeded 2 million copies. The American police made use of divination in their search for the notorious "Boston strangler."

We find that those who have had dealings with these practises often have to be delivered by the power of God from their influences. A woman began to develop pains in her chest which were very puzzling. She remembered that as a small girl she had been taken to a fortune-teller who had predicted that she would have a serious illness at that age, and that it would be in the area of her chest. Through prayer this evil power was cut off, and the pains immediately left her body. This is one example of many that could be given of the dangerous influences of divination.

The Cults

"The chaos of the cults" is a title of a book, and well it describes the position today. Much of the Church has been so uncertain of its message that it has lost the support of many sincere seekers. "If the bugle gives an indistinct sound, who will get ready for battle?" wrote Paul (1 Cor. 14:8). People are tired of pious platitudes; they want faith that works. Many have fallen for the cults, with their alluring promises, simple but dogmatic creeds, and easy conditions. Soka Gakkai is only one of many claiming the allegiance of the world. There are Jehovah's Witnesses, with their carefully worked out prophecies, Christian Science, with its promise of health, and Spiritualism with its "proof" of survival after death and its claims to contact dead loved ones. There is Rosicrucianism, Theosophy, Unity, Swedenborgianism, Christodelphianism, Mormonism, Baha'-ism and many others. In more recent times we have seen the birth of Scientology which, so its leaders claim, "revolutionises your character and gets rid of tensions and inhibitions." According to David McInnes,[7]

> It reinforces with wild promises all those things in which godless man loves to rest his confidence—technology, psychology and groundless optimism that everything will turn out all right in the end. It bolsters man's dreams of being able to cope by himself and to free himself from his problems by his own resources.

Spiritualism

We have already been through the biblical evidence which shows conclusively that all forms of spiritualism are forbidden to the people of God. But this particular act of disobedience seems particularly a source of temptation to the Church, uncertain as it has been about the question of life after death. There has been in the last fifty years a marked rise in spiritualism, particularly because of the First World War, when so many young widows were attracted to it through the opportunity they thought it would give them of contacting their loved ones lost in the war. Coupled with this was a growing interest in healing within the churches, and spiritualism has its own claims to healing power.

Here the Church of England has stumbled in its leadership. When a Commission was set up before the Second World War to look into this matter, its findings were never published. In 1969 the then bishop of Southwark, Dr. Mervyn Stockwood, wrote two articles in *The Times* on the subject of spiritualism. The second he entitled, "Can we communicate with the dead?" From the gist of what he wrote it is clear that he believes we can, although there is much chicanery too. But he ought not to have entitled the article, " *May* we communicate with the dead?" The answer to that question is a categorical no, according to the word of God and the teaching of the main stream of the Church right down to the present century. There is a clear "no entry" sign here, and Christian leadership is at fault if it tampers with the notice in any way. The *Oxford Dictionary of the Christian Church* states,[8] "the practise of spiritualism is denounced by scripture and by all parts of the Christian Church."

In the last few years I have heard of or personally counselled hundreds of people who have suffered in some way or other, in some cases very seriously, from dabbling or actively engaging in spiritualism. In the book *Between Christ and Satan,* the author, Dr. Kurt Koch, has conducted a very thorough survey and quotes hundreds of cases of those he himself has ministered to whose lives have been harmed by spiritualism. Many people who are engaged in spiritualism may be sincere. But sincerity is no defence against the delusions of Satan. Some allow for the human element of fraud but make no allowance for the work of deceiving spirits, who are well able to impersonate the dead. To be involved in any way in spiritualism is to open oneself to deceptive forces, and every Christian must keep well away. Nor is this a field for "research." The works of darkness are not to be investigated but reproved.

Attempts have been made by some to justify contacting the dead on the grounds of the experience of our Lord and the disciples on the Mount of Transfiguration. But this occasion bears no relationship to spiritualism whatsoever, and it has nothing in common with a seance. Luke gives us the main clue to what happened when he writes, "two men talked with him, Moses and Elijah, who appeared *in glory* and spoke of his departure, which he was to accomplish at Jerusalem" (Luke

9:30-31). They were not present there as "spirits," but in their glorified bodies. There was something unique too about the deaths of these two servants of God. In the case of Moses, we are told that God buried him (Deut. 34:6), and that the devil disputed about his body (Jude 9). In the case of Elijah, he was translated directly into heaven. To use this as an argument in favour of spiritualism, in the light of the mass of contrary evidence, is certainly clutching at a straw.

Morals

This revival of spiritual wickedness and deception is also taking place at a time of the most serious moral decay. Man is claiming the right not only to believe anything however contrary to reason, but also to do anything. Our permissive society claims no moral absolutes. Some of the modern teenage gods and goddesses are drug-takers and flagrantly promiscuous. There are no rules or standards. Sex is safer outside the boundaries of marriage, for modern marriage does not last.

Homosexuality and lesbianism grow and claim their freedom. Homosexuals in the United States claim to be the second largest minority after the blacks, and they are demanding freedom to solicit on the streets and in the public bars. Amsterdam is the homosexual capital of Europe, and many travel there every week from Britain in order to indulge in this perversion. Not content with their own depravity, there are some in society who would slander the righteous and even blasphemously drag Christ down to their level. In Rome in 1963 the play *Christo 1963* displayed our Lord's Crucifixion as a drunken orgy. Christ smells of alcohol, and Mary Magdalene who bends over Him is an unreformed prostitute.

Together with this throwing off of restraints is the alarming rise throughout the Western world of drug-taking, which together with alcoholism is contributing more and more to the rise in crime, road accidents, suicide, mental illness, promis- cuity and abortion. The rise in figures does not tell the whole story of misery and depravity which is resulting from the present climate of permissiveness, which is really another form of rebellion against God. The Church seems so utterly powerless in the face of all this. Soka Gakkai mockingly says, "Christianity is a religion without power."

Another aspect of all this is the deterioration of mental health in this country. According to a report of the Mental Health Research Fund in 1967, a quarter of Britain's adults are socially handicapped by psychiatric symptoms. Every year 27 million days are lost in industry due to depression and nervous disorders (a dozen times more than the time lost in strikes), and the National Health Service bill for tranquillisers and pep pills runs at £130 million a year. Family doctors treat more than 400,000 mentally troubled a year.

But Christianity has not always been a religion without power. There was a time when almost every Christian knew what it meant to have the power which had been promised by our Lord. And is it likely that in the face of "the devil's Pentecost" God is going to delay or default altogether in re-equipping his Church with powers to go again into action against those evil powers behind so much of the evil and misery of the world today?

In some cases missionaries are being sent abroad into strongly held enemy territory unarmed, unprotected and largely untrained for spiritual warfare. No wonder there is such a high casualty rate, with so many returning disheartened, depressed or ill. The situation at home is similar. Many Christian leaders and workers, who began their ministry full of hope and zeal, are now a shadow of the people they once were. They have been gradually worn down by hard and often fruitless work, not fully understanding the real nature of the battle, nor how to win through against what often appears impossible odds. A modern general would be instantly dismissed if he dared to send such unprepared soldiers into battle against such a skilful and merciless enemy!

Professor Harvey Cox has written a book with the title *On Not Leaving It to the Snake*. He takes the theme that evil triumphs when the good do nothing. Herein lies the failure of the Church. In doing so little, evil has triumphed. It is up to us to reverse all this. The first part of this book has been concerned to make plain the battle we are engaged in, so that we can see and recognise who the real enemy is. The second part is concerned with how to deal with him, and how to win the battle for ourselves and others. By now, one trusts, we are all convinced recruits, even if a little raw. We will find that the God who enlists us in his army will also train us. As King David put it, "he trains my hands for war and my fingers for battle."

II

The Fight of Faith

Fight the good fight of the faith.
1 Tim. 1:6-12

SIX

These Things

THE FIRST PART OF THE BOOK has been concerned with detecting Satan's work, in discovering where and how he works. The second part is chiefly taken up with the kind of action that should follow such discoveries.

This may be seen in terms of resistance, when Satan seeks to enter a situation. It may be through sowing doubts or fears into our minds, or sickness into our bodies. This is the most normal area of temptation. "Resist the devil," James tells us (4:7), "and he will flee from you." But note that this promise is prefaced by the words "submit yourselves therefore to God." A woman once told a minister that she did not believe the truth of this text; "when I resist the devil," she told him, "he flies at me." He wisely asked her if her life was truly submitted to God, for the enemy only flees when this is so. It is one of the most exhilarating experiences in life to discover that this promise is true, and that the devil is not omnipotent, but has to go when told to. "Resist him," writes Peter (1 Peter 5:8), "firm in your faith."

But different treatment is required when Satan has actually gained access to our lives. It is no good resisting him when he is "in residence," so-to-speak. We must serve him immediately with an eviction order, but the measure of success we have may well depend to a greater or lesser extent on the people we are, the use of the weapons God has placed in our hands, and the procedure we follow. Detection is half the battle, but expulsion must follow, and we must be prepared to persevere until the enemy leaves for good.

In some ways my wife and I stumbled on this ministry. It opened up to us through personal experience. God presented us with unlikely and testing situations which compelled us to take action. It was all so very unexpected when the first test came.

I was woken up in the early hours of the morning by the sound of the telephone. I clambered bleary-eyed from bed, wondering who on earth would be calling us at such an hour. The man on the other end was a personal friend, and he urgently pleaded with me to set him free from evil powers, which, he said, were tormenting him at that very moment. Only a year or so before I would have dismissed the whole business as some kind of mental disturbance, promised to pray for the person (and probably forgotten to do so), and gone quickly back to bed. But I had just become vividly aware of spiritual warfare, so that I had to take this call seriously.

There and then over the telephone I exercised the authority which a Christian has. In the name of Jesus I rebuked these powers and commanded them to leave my friend. Only when he acknowledged they had gone did I ring off and return to bed. So a new ministry was born, and from time to time ever since my wife and I have come face to face with similar needs and situations. It has not often needed a "casting out," but on many occasions it has resulted in the person being wonderfully released from satanic power and bondage.

We have found too that it does bring a sense of reality, and is seldom really a source of embarrassment. I was speaking once in an Anglican church hall. When I finished I asked for silent prayer, and the atmosphere was unusually charged with the atmosphere of the Holy Spirit. Suddenly the stillness was broken by a woman who began to cry out. She was moaning as if in pain, and turned and clutched the person sitting next to her, at the same time gradually slipping from her chair and finishing up lying on the floor. There was no time for discussion! Some action was called for. It was clearly an attack of Satan, so the spirit was bound and cast out in the name of Jesus—right in full view of the audience.

Being the first meeting of a weekend visit to this church, and knowing that there were many visitors from neighbouring churches present, I was rather apprehensive about the impression that had been created by this unusual incident. Shortly after the meeting had been dismissed, a leader from another church approached me. He confessed that he had come to the meeting full of scepticism about the charismatic renewal, and that it was not until this incident took place that he had altered his opinion. But when this happened he could no longer doubt the reality of the supernatural.

We ministered to this woman afterwards and discovered that she was a quiet and undemonstrative person who normally was unforthcoming at public meetings. We laid hands on her and she was filled with the Holy Spirit, her response this time being wholly different from the previous occasion.

So we discovered ways in which God moves in people's lives to free them from the power of Satan. It was true also of the disciples, who discovered for themselves, without Jesus' direct instructions, the nature of spiritual warfare and the way of victory. For when Jesus sent the Seventy on ahead of Him, his commission to them was somewhat different from that of the Twelve. They were told to heal the sick (Luke 10:9), but there was no mention of power and authority over "all demons," which He had specifically delegated to the Twelve (9:1).

The Seventy, however, exceeded themselves, and even their commission, for they made the discovery that "even the demons are subject to us in your name!" Jesus did not rebuke them for going beyond their orders. But He cautioned them against the danger of pride. The source of a Christian's joy should be in his status not his success. There is no doubt a two-fold thought in his words, "I saw Satan fall like lightning from heaven." On the one hand there is the *cause* of that fall, the pride that consumed Satan; the disciples were in the same danger, flushed as they were with their success, of falling from grace, and so Christ issued them with this warning. "There are few Christians," writes Bishop J.C. Ryle, "who can carry a full cup with a steady hand."

There followed from the lips of Jesus an authorisation and a promise which still today form one of the foundation stones of spiritual warfare, "I have given you authority to tread upon serpents and scorpions and over all the power of the enemy; and nothing shall hurt you." The verb "I have given" is in the perfect tense, and there is no exact equivalent in English. It describes the present result of a past action. The authority that is given by Christ is meant to bring about results, and this is very important, as we shall be seeing.

But even more significant is what followed. We are told that Jesus at the same time "rejoiced in the Holy Spirit." Although we are told three times in the gospels that Jesus wept, this is the only occasion that we are told that He rejoiced. It must be important! Of course, He must have rejoiced many times, for He was, according to prophecy, "anointed with the oil of gladness above his fellows" (Heb. 1:9 quoting Ps. 45:7). But the Holy Spirit is saying something very important here if it is the only recorded instance of this rejoicing.

The cause of this outburst of praise was the fact that "these things," hidden from the wise and understanding, had been revealed to babes. But what were "these things"? In the context it clearly refers to the revelation made to the disciples of the unseen world. The fact that their names were written in heaven and that they had authority over the unseen powers of the devil—the fact that Satan had fallen from heaven, and that their names were inscribed there! Things that could only be understood and experienced by revelation.

It is this revelation that is so desperately needed by Christians today. It is *the* issue we face. It is the fact asserted constantly by Christ and the apostles that "flesh and blood shall not inherit the kingdom of God" and that "we are not contending against flesh and blood, but against the principalities, against the powers, against the world rulers of this present darkness, against the spiritual hosts of wickedness in the heavenly places." Not too pretty a picture of entrenched evil! We do not see much of this on the surface. The devil can disguise himself as an angel of light. As Merril F. Unger has put it, "with the crude savage Satan may best accomplish his purpose as a roaring lion—with the cultured and educated he can work more effectively as an angel of light."[10] Satan is a past master at being indigenous. His work can look very respectable—on the surface. But behind the facade is immense power, vulnerable only to the authority of a Christian who believes in the power of the name of Jesus Christ. No wonder Jesus rejoiced when He heard how the disciples had overthrown some of this evil, and found that his name brought these powers into subjection. The work of the gospel takes place on this battleground. Evangelism is a part of this giant rescue operation of God in a world which is "in the power of the evil one" (1 John 5:9). Our work is to turn men "from the power of Satan to God" (Acts 26:18).

Revelation must lead to action.

SEVEN

The Overcomers

IF WE ARE TO JUDGE by the letters of Christ to the seven churches (Revelation 2-3), then Christians in the big cities of Asia Minor were faced with the same kind of spiritual warfare that this book describes. In Smyrna and Philadelphia there were "synagogues of Satan." In Pergamum there was Satan's throne, and the city was described as "where Satan dwells." In Thyatira there was a woman, maybe a spiritist medium, who was teaching "the deep things of Satan." At the end of each letter Jesus promised blessings to "him that overcometh" (A.V.). So this chapter is about "the overcomers"—those who have learned how to defeat Satan, and how to free others from his attacks.

It is an interesting and revealing fact that there is no mention of the office of "exorcist" in the various lists given us in the New Testament. There are "healers," "evangelists" and "prophets," but apparently no exorcists. It is not until very much later that they are mentioned in a list of so-called "minor orders," in a letter of Bishop Cornelius of Rome to Fabius of Antioch in 252 A.D. The *Oxford Dictionary of the Christian Church*[11] quite rightly says that the power of exorcising evil spirits "was never confined to the member of a particular order." The office is now extinct in the Western Church, and in the Eastern "exorcism is regarded as a charismatic gift not attached to an office." In the New Testament exorcism is a ministry which is potentially available to every Christian. In Mark 16:17 Jesus asserts that the casting out of evil spirits is one of the signs which will follow "them that believe"; and although He did not actually commission the Seventy to exorcise, He rejoiced, as we saw in the last chapter, when they did it.

Again, we notice that it was Philip, a "layman" as some would call him, who cast many evil spirits out of the Samaritans (Acts 8). There is no ground for thinking that God ever intended this important ministry to be restricted to a particular group of people, and certainly not to an official "priesthood." But this does not mean to say that any Tom, Dick or Harry may exercise this ministry, as the sons of Sceva discovered to their cost (Acts 19).

As far as the Church of England is concerned, the position is governed by Canon Law. Technically it requires the Bishop's permission before any exorcism can be carried out. It is best, if one is an ordained minister of the Church of England, to obtain a general permission to carry on this ministry, reporting from time to time to the Bishop the results as they come. No Bishop is going to thank you if you are constantly seeking his permission for a ministry which, in any case, may need to be exercised without delay. Nevertheless, some control is very necessary. Experience in recent years has shown that a good deal of harm can be caused by zealous people acting without due thought, consideration or humility. There are safeguards that need to be taken. It is dangerous work. You might just as well sell gelignite over the counter without any restrictions as let anyone loose with the authority to exorcise. Control is best exercised in the local church. Bishops and other church leaders do not have the time to keep tabs on this kind of ministry, and, if the truth be known, some do not believe in the existence of evil spirits anyway! Every local church should bring this ministry under the general surveillance of its particular disciplines. Only people whom the leaders respect and regard as suitable should be permitted to exercise such a ministry amongst church members. Ministers should pray that God will raise up people, properly qualified, who can fulfil it.

Care should be exercised when itinerant speakers arrive on

the scene, or in the area with a claim to such a ministry. They may be sound and helpful, but their credentials should be examined, for some trouble in the past has been caused by "demon chasers" who leave behind them considerable confusion. It is not only significant that there were no Christian exorcists mentioned in the New Testament, but also that there were no "deliverance centres" specialising in this ministry. In recent years they have sprung up in England, on the Continent of Europe, and in the United States, and show signs of aberration of one kind or another. We can only conclude from the biblical evidence that God never really intended any of his people to specialise in this exacting ministry. It is much better and more healthy when the whole body of Christ is concerned, and when those who are called to this ministry within the local church are integrated into the rest of the fellowship. We are to be "babes in evil." As David du Plessis has put it, "Don't go around looking for demons. But if you find them, *tread on them!*" This is a healthy attitude to adopt.

When the sons of Sceva, the Jewish high priest, saw Paul's success in this realm and heard him using the Christian formula of the name of Jesus, they thought they were bound to have the same results if they invoked the same name. But what followed revealed that it was not respect for Jesus' name alone that mattered, but also the quality of life of those who were using it. The demons had recognised Jesus—"Jesus we know," they said. "The demons believe and shudder," says James in his epistle. They knew Paul too. But the spirit world refused to recognise the authority of the name of Christ when it was used on the lips of the sons of Sceva. Instead of overcoming the demonic power, they themselves were attacked by the demon-possessed man, and even though they out-numbered him seven to one, he tore their clothes off them and sent them fleeing in terror from the place. Obviously the kind of people we are and the kind of life we live is going to count a lot in our warfare against demonic powers. What particular qualities should we expect to see in one who exercises this ministry successfully?

Purity

Without discernment this ministry will be seriously hampered, and without purity of life discernment will be unreliable. In detecting, opposing and overcoming evil power, we need to be pure ourselves. Jesus once said, "If your eye is sound, your whole body will be full of light; but if your eye is not sound, your whole body will be full of darkness" (Matt. 7:22-23). Or if we are looking for a small piece of sawdust in someone else's eye, while our own has a beam of wood in it, then we shall not be able to help the other person. We must have the beam removed first and then, Jesus says, "you will see clearly to take the speck out of your brother's eye" (Matt. 7:3-5).

The one who is free to move unmolested into enemy territory is the one who has a passion for righteousness and a hatred of evil; while a person who hankers after illicit pleasures, does Christian work for his own advantage, is undisciplined in his daily life, or is constantly self-indulgent will seldom be used to deliver others; on the contrary he may well be a stumbling-block to the other person's release and might well become a victim of the very thing from which he is trying to release the other person. Paul kept his body disciplined at all times, "lest after preaching to others I myself should be disqualified" (1 Cor. 9:27).

This purity should extend to our motives and desires also. Our chief desire should always be the glory of God, not our own. It is not always easy to keep it that way. The dangers of pride are particularly relevant to this ministry. We saw how Jesus recognised the danger of this when the Seventy returned with such success, proving for the first time the power and authority of Jesus' name. The scent of victory was in their nostrils when Jesus had to say to them: "nevertheless do not rejoice in this, that the demons are subject to you in my name, but rather that your names are written in heaven." It is easy to see the subtlety of this temptation when we realise that it is a delegated ministry. It is true that its success is dependent on God and the powerful name of his Son. But the authority is exercised by us. We do the binding and loosing. It is much harder to give the glory to God when one is so involved oneself in the actual ministry and its outcome. A constant searching of our hearts is necessary to see if there is any human pride lurking there, for if there is, then the ministry will quickly lose its effectiveness. Humility must always be the key-note. Without Jesus' victory at Calvary, it would be impossible to defeat these spiritual powers anyway.

But we also need to watch our motives with regard to the people we minister to. We may be involved in matters of a personal nature relating to the one in need of help. Our motive should be the person's good. It should be based on the motive of love and compassion, a real concern for the person as such. It must never be our wish to hurt, shame or embarrass such people, or to be inquisitive, delving into their private life. The secrets of the heart are a sacred trust. It is vital that confidences are kept and that we do not share them with anyone else without their permission. People will seldom confide in us if there is any likelihood of our abusing their confidences; and very often such deep confiding is essential for a full release to be secured. We need to uphold constantly the sanctity of human life.

It is not only true that the pure in heart "see God," but they are often able to see deeply into the lives of others. But true spiritual discernment should never be divorced from holy living. Without self-discipline and Christ-like living, there will be little lasting success in this ministry.

We do need to learn more about the value of fasting and the place it should have in our life and ministry. Fasting has been much neglected by all sections of the Church.

Power

Although the disciples overcame Satan and cast out demons before Pentecost, they were much more successful and dis-cerning after they had been filled with the Holy Spirit. So today it is possible to minister without being filled with the Spirit, but for its fullest implementation this power is essential. The pentecostal blessing normally leads us into a fuller charismatic ministry, and the gifts of the Spirit are very important. The power of the Holy Spirit usually gives a heightened sense and awareness of the powers of evil and the conflict involved with them, and Satan usually attacks more viciously and thus lays bare his stratagems. We are made much more aware of the supernatural and the warfare that is going on in the "heavenly places." Moreover the gift of speaking in unknown languages, which often accompanied the receiving of the Spirit in New Testament times, is invaluable when dealing with the attacks of Satan.

In the magazine *Renewal,*[12] the Rev. Malcolm Piper drew attention to this interesting factor. In Ephesians 6:17 Paul speaks of "the sword of the Spirit which is the word of God." F. Foulkes in a footnote in his Tyndale commentary says,[13] "the reference is not only to Scripture, but to all 'words that come from God' (NEB) by his Spirit." The term used for "word" here (*rhema*) signifies the word as spoken. This can, therefore, refer to speaking in tongues, for in Acts 2:4 the gift is described as "the Spirit giving them the words to utter" (Weymouth). This is confirmed by the verse that follows which refers to using "every kind of prayer and intreaty, and at every opportunity pray in the Spirit" (Goodspeed). In fact, many are finding the gift of speaking in tongues more and more helpful in spiritual warfare. Brother Andrew, whose exciting story of Bible smuggling is told in *God's Smuggler,*[14] has said, "so far as speaking in tongues is concerned . . . I find it indispensable when crossing the communist borders with Bibles." This gift was used by God again and again to deliver people from drug addiction in the work of David Wilkerson in New York, which has been made famous by *The Cross and the Switchblade.*"[15] Such a powerful weapon should not be neglected.

Authority

There was an occasion when the disciples were unsuccessful in casting out an evil spirit. Jesus attributed this to their unbelief, and possibly lack of prayer and fasting. Belief and authority go closely together. Jesus has given us authority "to tread upon serpents and scorpions and over all the power of the enemy" (Luke 10:19), but unless this authority is faithfully exercised, nothing will happen. Authority is faith in action. Authority will give us that persistence that refuses to take no for an answer, and continues to command the enemy until he has to give way.

One of the greatest needs today is for believers to recognise and exercise the authority they have through the name of the Lord Jesus Christ. God has delegated this authority to us to exercise, and it is foolish if we pass it back to Him. *Many of our problems are caused because we are constantly doing things that God has said He will do, and because we expect God to do things He has told us to do.* It is like playing doubles at tennis. One of the best shots is to hit the ball midway between the two partners. Either both will try to hit it, or they will both leave the shot to their partner to play. When the "ball" goes between God's court and ours, we need to know whether to play it ourselves, or leave it to God. As far as casting out spirits and exercising dominion over Satan are concerned, God says "yours," and we have to play the shot accordingly. *We have the authority.* The centurion, in the gospel story, knew what authority meant. He had this delegated to him from above. He told those under him "to do this" and they did it. He could never exercise such authority if he himself were not likewise under the authority of his senior officers, and so on right up the ranks to Caesar himself. The ultimate authority came from Caesar, but the centurion issued the orders, and they were obeyed. It would obviously be ludicrous if whenever the centurion wanted something done he had to ask Caesar to issue the commands! So it is with us. We give Satan and evil spirits their orders to leave, and *they have to obey*, for our lives are under the sovereign power of God Himself. When the demons mutinied on the sons of Sceva, it was because they had not been authorised by Jesus Christ to use his name. If we are true Christians, born of his Spirit, then we have this authorisation. What an exciting moment it is when we see the enemy fleeing at the name of Jesus! No wonder the Seventy returned with joy after such experiences.

Knowledge of the Word

When we serve someone with a writ we have to be careful to see that it is a proper legal document. This is especially true when we are dealing with a legal expert ourselves. So when we give Satan his notice to quit, we must be sure that the law is on our side. Satan is a past master at this kind of "litigation." He knows how to argue his way out of anything. But when Jesus encountered Satan in the wilderness, He proved himself the master advocate, for He knew the word better than Satan. He was able to quote it with accuracy and authority.

This is of fundamental importance in tackling the enemy. As we have seen, we are basically involved with the "father of lies," whose main tool is deceit. He has been "a liar from the beginning," and he will lie to the end. We must know the truth as it is revealed to us in the scriptures. It is no coincidence that the greatest in-road of satanic deception through the cults has taken place at the same time as modernism has undermined man's confidence in the word of God. If we depart from this standard, we will be like a ship breaking from its moorings in a gale. We will be blown hither and thither, or, as Paul describes it, "tossed to and fro and carried about with every wind of doctrine, by the cunning of men, by their craftiness in deceitful wiles" (Eph. 4:14). Without this anchor we will inevitably suffer shipwreck.

We have already seen how spiritualism has to be rejected altogether because it is forbidden in the word of God. Such an approach is not very popular in these so-called "enlightened" days. We may be dubbed "fundamentalists." But so they vilified the prophets and men of God of all ages, who have stood firm for truth against many forms of error.

In the third chapter of Malachi the prophet called God's people to put their house in order. They are to allow God to refine and purify them. They are to return to Him. They are not tithing their possessions. They are careless and not walking uprightly. Reading such verses one becomes more and more familiar with modern Christianity! The prophet is very up-to-date. But God promises blessings to those who repent and put their house in order.

Repentance is a key to discernment and authority in dealing with Satan. God has to wait for a full repentance. And then what follows? Malachi tells us—"*then* once more you shall distinguish between the righteous and the wicked, between one who serves God and one who does not serve Him" (3:18). This is the kind of discrimination which is so urgently needed. It is a disturbing thought that the kind of people we are will radically affect, more than in any other field, our effectiveness or otherwise in detecting the power and presence of the enemy and delivering people from his influence. If this is so, then we must constantly be open to the convicting work of the Holy Spirit, revealing the subtle as well as the more obvious sins and shortcomings. Then we shall be able to look with pure eyes on the affairs of others. And to such, God gives his very powerful weapons, of which we shall be writing in the next chapter.

EIGHT

Our Weapons

T O LEAD A PERSON TO CHRIST and not to show him how he can
be filled with the Holy Spirit is like recruiting someone for
the army and not providing him with adequate weapons. If he
goes to war unarmed, and unprotected for that matter, he will
make little impression on the enemy, and likely as not will finish
up a casualty or a prisoner of war. Jesus himself made sure that
his disciples did not commence battle until they had been filled
with the Holy Spirit and equipped with spiritual gifts, and He
offers the same resources to us.

There are many kinds of weapons in God's armoury, and the
Christian soldier needs to be acquainted with each of them.
There are some that are offensive weapons, others used for
defence. Some to neutralise the enemy, others to protect
ourselves from his attacks. Paul describes them well in this way:

It is true that I am an ordinary weak human being, but I don't
use human plans and methods to win my battles. I use God's
mighty weapons, not those made by men, to knock down the
devil's strongholds. These weapons can break down every
proud argument against God and every wall that can be built
to keep men from finding him. With these weapons I can
capture rebels and bring them back to God, and change them
into men whose heart's desire is obedience to Christ.

2 Cor. 10:3-5

The Name

No one reading the New Testament can escape the crucial nature of the name of Jesus in every part of it. Let us list some of its uses:

Salvation —"there is no other name under heaven given among men by which we must be saved" Acts 4:12 (see also 9:21, 10:43 and John 1:12)

Justification —"you were justified in the name of the Lord Jesus Christ and in the Spirit of our God" 1 Cor. 6:11

Healing —"in the name of Jesus Christ of Nazareth walk" Acts 3:6

Preaching —"Philip preached good news about the kingdom of God and the name of Jesus Christ" Acts 8:12 (see also 9:27)

Exorcism —"I charge you in the name of Jesus Christ to come out of her" Acts 16:18 (see also Mark 16:17)

Church discipline —"I have already pronounced judgment in the name of the Lord Jesus on the man who has done such a thing" 1 Cor. 5:3-4

Worship —"always and for everything giving thanks in the name of our Lord Jesus Christ to God the Father" Eph. 5:20

Prayer —"whatever you ask in my name, I will do it, that the Father may be glorified in the Son; if you ask anything in my name, I will do it" John 14:13-14

The gift of the Holy Spirit —"but the Counsellor, the Holy Spirit, whom the Father will send in my name, he will teach you all things. . ." John 14:26

Persecution —"then they left the presence of the council, rejoicing that they were counted worthy to suffer dishonour for the name." Acts 5:41 (see also Matt. 5:41, Matt. 24:9 and Acts 9:16)

It can all be summarised by the words of Paul, "Whatever you do, in word or deed, do everything in the name of the Lord Jesus" (Col. 3:17).

You could not have a more comprehensive injunction than that! The name of Jesus, however, is not to be used as a kind of lucky talisman, and there is nothing magical about the word itself. In Acts 19, as we have already seen, the sons of Sceva tried to use it this way with painful results. But from Pentecost onwards the name of Jesus figures very prominently in the whole forward movement of the Christian Church.

The name of a person in both the Old and New Testaments means very much more than the word itself. It means the entire person, his attributes, personality and power. We recognise the same in everyday life. A cheque without a signature is only worth the paper it is printed on. It all depends on that name at the bottom right-hand corner. That signature or name represents that person's financial resources and the part of them which he is prepared to part with. It is as if Jesus left behind Him a cheque book full of blank cheques which He has signed with his name. The believer fills in the amount as the will of God is revealed, and the cheque once presented is met by the inexhaustible riches of Christ. So through the name of Jesus, some believe, others receive the Holy Spirit, others are healed and others are delivered from satanic power. How tragic when we use the cheque book of our own resources and find the cheques are always bouncing! God's cheques, when signed with the name of Jesus, are always honoured.

When we use the name of Jesus we are recognising the fact that we are not ministering in our own name or for our own blessing. We are acting as his representatives. When people accept Christ through our witness, or are healed through the laying on of hands, or set free through the ministry of exorcism, then it is Christ who has ministered. He has met with these people, and we have only been his representatives and means. As we invoke the name of Jesus, we are bringing that person into his presence that He might minister to them. We must also guard jealously the glory and honour of Jesus' name, and see that none is given or received by ourselves.

The name of Jesus is a powerful weapon in our hands, and since we are to do everything in that name it should often be on our lips and in our prayers. We must always use it reverently and discreetly. We must never want to become so familiar with it that we lose the sense of awe and wonder that surrounds it. It is the name to which one day every knee will bow and every tongue have to confess. We must bow to that name *now*, and confess it boldly and believingly, and as we pray for others according to their need, let us use it firmly and confidently.

The Word of God

This weapon has already been mentioned in the previous chapter. It is the one offensive weapon referred to in the famous passage on spiritual warfare in Ephesians 6. The armour is for protection, but the sword of the Spirit "which is the word of God" is useful for both attack and defence. In Hebrews 4:12 the word of God is again likened to a sword—it is "alive and active. It cuts more keenly than any two-edged sword, piercing as far as the place where life and spirit, joints and marrow, divide. It sifts the purposes and thoughts of the heart" (NEB).

There is nothing quite like the word of God, proclaimed in the power of the Holy Spirit, for forcing the enemy into the open and revealing the presence of Satan's influence. Martin Luther recognised this, as part of a verse of one of his famous hymns reveals:

And let the prince of ill
Look grim as e'er he will,
He harms us not a whit,
For why?—his doom is writ;
A word shall quickly slay him.

No doubt too this is the explanation for the experiences of the early Methodists. For when John Wesley and others began to preach in some places, strong people would begin to cry out, sometimes manifesting the symptoms of epilepsy. There is no more powerful combination than that of the Spirit and word of God. When mixed in the right proportions the enemy is sure to be exposed and overthrown.

But the word of God is not only an irritant, it also heals and strengthens. It has been said of preaching that it should "disturb the comfortable and comfort the disturbed." This aptly describes the ministry of the word. When we are counselling and trying to help people who are oppressed by satanic power, we must know how to apply the word of God not only in diagnosing the cause of the trouble, but also in prescribing the remedy. Mrs. Jean Darnall has devised a very helpful method in this respect. She calls it "scriptural prescriptions," and like medicine they are to be taken by the patient "three times a day." We simply write out for the one we are trying to help (or for ourselves if we are treating ourselves!) a set of relevant scriptures. It is then suggested that these be read aloud three times, morning, noon and before going to bed. First, they are spoken to God, as witness that He has written this and so will fulfil it; secondly, to ourselves, as witnessing to the fact that it applies to us and we believe it; and thirdly, to the devil, as Jesus did in the wilderness, so that he has eventually to flee.

Righteousness

Paul regarded this as a weapon as well as part of the Christian armour to protect him from attack (i.e., the breastplate of righteousness). In 2 Corinthians 6:6, he refers to "the weapons of righteousness for the right hand and for the left." It seems as if we should be ambidextrous in our spiritual warfare! Ready for anything! But Paul probably means here "weapons for enemies all round us."

In the context of 2 Corinthians 6, from which this text comes, Paul is defending himself from the misrepresentation and obloquy of his Christian opponents in Corinth, who wanted to exalt others over Paul. His ministry and life had been seriously criticised, and he is at pains to point out the features which commended them, and this is one of them.

Our ministry, if it is anything like that of Christ's and Paul's, will inevitably meet with criticism, and even be strongly opposed. This is especially true when we have been filled with the Holy Spirit, begin to exercise a charismatic ministry, and find that people are somewhat sceptical of our new enthusiasm. We will find Christians looking askance at us. Some will take it upon themselves to obstruct us. Others will sit uncomfortably on the proverbial fence, scrutinising all that we do. But Paul recognised the importance of a good conscience. Whatever people may say about us, we must see that before God we are innocent. We have to be especially careful about money. We need to be able to echo the words of Paul: "I coveted no one's silver or gold or apparel" (Acts 20:33). Paul tells Timothy that his aim was a "good conscience" as well as "sincere faith" (1 Tim. 1:5). He also urges Timothy in waging the spiritual warfare to have faith and "a good conscience" (1 Tim. 1:19). For there were some who had made shipwreck of their faith by jettisoning their consciences. Faith and a good conscience should always go together. Paul draws them together again (1 Tim. 3:9), and warns about those whose consciences had been seared (literally "burnt with a hot iron"). Conscience alone is not a safe guide, and this is the reason why Paul usually attaches an adjective to it—"good" or "clear" (2 Tim. 1:3) or "void of offence" (Acts 24:16).

Righteousness, then, is a powerful weapon in our hands. But it is not our righteousness that counts but rather that which comes "through faith in Christ, the righteousness from God that depends on faith" (Phil. 3:9). Proverbs 10 is a fine passage to read, since it lists the blessings that come to those who have this gift.

Spiritual Gifts

The return of the *charismata* in our generation, on a scale never before experienced, is one of the most important factors in the contemporary Church situation. For it means that weapons are being re-discovered which, put to proper use, could swing the pendulum strongly in the right direction and be the means of drawing millions back to God and his kingdom.

It is not the purpose of this book to give a detailed explanation of these gifts, but to draw attention to the three which are particularly appropriate—"the word of wisdom," "the word of knowledge," and "the discerning of spirits." The first two are often paired together. They are the means of conveying to us inspired understanding of situations and of people's needs.

The best examples of the operation of the gift of the "word of wisdom" can be found in the inspired way in which our Lord answered his hecklers. There were times when many present must have thought it impossible for Him to answer the questions put to Him without falling into the trap that had deliberately been set. "Fetch me a coin" was just such a "word of wisdom," in answer to the awkward question about whether it was right to pay taxes to Caesar or not. And we can expect the same help from the Holy Spirit when placed in awkward situations.

To give you a modern example, a minister was facing the danger of division in his church when some of the members were being filled with the Holy Spirit and receiving charismatic gifts. Others in the church resented what was happening. One of them expressed his concern to the minister after a Sunday service. "It stamps us second-class Christians," he alleged, adding sarcastically, "and they're a queer lot for all that." "Well," said the minister in reply, "perhaps they need it more than you do." It was the perfect answer—a word of wisdom. It pacified an irate church member, who very soon was rejoicing in the same blessing himself.

Jesus often manifested the companion gift—the word of knowledge. In the days of his life on earth He was given, on many occasions, supernatural pieces of information which proved invaluable to his ministry. He knew, for example, the real need of the woman at the well of Sychar, and that she had been married five times. He knew exactly when "the hour" had come. He "saw" Nathaniel under the fig tree before He had ever met him.

And the Holy Spirit gives this gift today. It is particularly useful when trying to help people who have had damaging experiences in early childhood, which they cannot themelves remember and which they may have repressed. A woman was being prayed for, with deep needs affecting her physically as well as spiritually. Suddenly one of those present, who hardly knew her, described a toy pet. Immediately memories came back of a serious deprivation when a small girl of a much loved toy. Healing followed the release of this amongst other memories during prayer and the laying on of hands. Another example concerns a young man at a conference. In a time of prayer someone shared a vision, which exactly described some of this man's past life, and revealed the basis of fears which had hindered his spiritual development and prevented him from witnessing freely. Later that evening the fear was dealt with and a new release experienced.

Jesus, of course, had this gift of "discerning of spirits" and manifested it on many occasions. It is a gift of discrimination, and indispensable in spiritual warfare. It helps us to distinguish between various possible agencies and to discover the true source and motivation of life and action. Jesus' ability is described as "He knew what was in man" (John 2:25). He was able to interpret human motives and assess the genuineness or otherwise of people's words and actions. He seemed instinctively to recognise hypocrisy on the one hand, and reality on the other. He knew when men had faith, and when they did not; when they were telling the truth and when they were lying. The "Word made flesh" was able to discern "the thoughts and intents of the heart" as the written word does according to Hebrews 4:12.

Since Jesus gives us the same commission as He received from the Father, anoints us with the same power, and promises that we will do the same works, it is not surprising when we read in the Acts of the Apostles that the disciples were equipped with the same discernment. Peter, for example, recognises the hypocrisy in Ananias and Sapphira (Acts 5:3), and exposes the wickedness of Simon Magus (Acts 8:30). Paul discerns the spirit of divination in the servant girl (Acts 16:17f), and so on.

The Holy Spirit desires, through the operation of this gift, to enable Christians to distinguish accurately between what comes from above," and what rises "from below." What comes from God, what comes from man, and what comes from Satan. In any given situation there may be a mixture, but the Holy Spirit will help us to analyse the situation and label the parts correctly.

Although these gifts are part of the "spirituals" (*pneumatikoi*), which means that they are given by the Holy Spirit and are not natural abilities, they will still be manifested in proportion to the spiritual development of the Christian. There is a need, as expressed in Hebrews 5:14, to have our faculties "trained by patience to distinguish good from evil." As with all the other gifts, practise is the surest way to learn. A humble attitude and a readiness to admit failure when it occurs are important factors in the learning process. If one is not able to distinguish clearly at the time, one is often able later to do so in the light of subsequent events. But we should expect to know at the time, and this will be our experience increasingly as time goes on.

There will be some to whom the secrets of this particular area of the kingdom will be revealed in greater degree than to others. This is not necessarily any reflection on either faithfulness or dedication. We need to recognise that there are different ministries in the body of Christ as well as gifts. Just as James in his epistle discourages people from becoming teachers (James 3:1), for they are to be judged with greater strictness, so naturally we shrink from the responsibility of this ministry of discernment. However, every Christian needs in some measure this gift, for we are constantly forced by circumstances to require it.

So much for our weapons. Now we must consider the important matter of our protection from the enemy's attacks.

NINE

Our Protection

EVERY CHRISTIAN NEEDS PROTECTION from enemy attacks, especially those engaged in violent spiritual warfare. The history of how man has gone to war down the centuries is largely a story of weapons improving in their potency, and armour increasing in its protectiveness. And Christians are vulnerable to attacks from the enemy and need the means to protect themselves. There are places and situations which Christians should not enter into recklessly or without the proper safeguards. In cases where exorcism is necessary, it is best to work with a partner. It is significant that Jesus always sent his disciples out in pairs, and the apostles mostly had a partner with them on their missionary journeys.

The Armour of God

The classic chapter on protection is Ephesians 6. Paul uses the armour that the Roman legionaries used to illustrate the means of protection that God has provided for the Christian. It is very important at the outset to grasp the fact that this is not *our* armour, but *God's*, given to us to protect us. It is not *our* righteousness, or *our* faith, or *our* gospel which can stand in the evil day. It is God's provision alone which will give us adequate protection. If we see this simple but profound fact it could well make all the difference between victory and defeat. And in a sense all the pieces of armour, when combined together, are Christ himself. Elsewhere Paul does urge his readers to "put on

Christ" (Gal. 3:27). He is our protector.

Notice too that we need to put on this armour *before* the battle. A fairly elementary point, but sometimes overlooked. It is no good waiting until the dart is on its way before holding up the shield of faith.

One of the best ways of considering the pieces of armour is to see them as protecting us from various points of attack, thus enabling the enemy's blows to glance off us and not penetrate. so with each piece we shall list the particular form of attack from which the armour protects us.

The girdle of truth. *Form of attack—lies and errors.* Satan has been a liar from the beginning and is the father of lies, Jesus tells us (John 8:44). The first attack he made on man took the form of a lie—"you shall not die," Satan said, in defiance of the fact that God had clearly said they would if they took the forbidden fruit. Someone has helpfully summarised the truth as "God is what He says He is; I am what God says I am; God does what He says He will do; I can do what God says I can do." Satan is always causing us to doubt these statements. "God can't be a God of love"; "God can't really be in control of the universe"; "I'm too sinful to be a child of God"; "My old nature can't possibly be dead"; "God can't save me from this predicament I'm in"; "I can't do it"; and so on. And Satan has always twisted and perverted the word of God.

One of the favourite forms of attacks on Christians is false accusation. He is called in Revelation "the accuser of the brethren," and he accuses us continuously before God (Rev. 12:10). He will never get God to believe these lies about us, but it is surprising how many of God's children are taken in. One of the most common complaints amongst Christians is self-despair, and far too often it comes from believing what Satan says about us rather than God. The armour to meet this attack is "the girdle of truth." When falsely condemned we declare the truth—"there is therefore now no condemnation for those who are in Christ Jesus" (Rom. 8:1). But we need to discern between the pricks of conscience, given to us by the Holy Spirit, and the nagging accusations of Satan. Here a "good and honest heart" is needed. Whilst we should always be open to correction by the Holy Spirit, let us not hold the door open so wide that we let Satan's accusations in too.

Equally powerful these days seems to be the maligning of God's character by Satan. How many Christians one meets who do not believe that God really loves them! As Job won through, when all the circumstances pointed in the opposite direction, and was able to say, "blessed be the name of the Lord," so we too will be helped to see disasters when they come as "blessings," rather than listen to the slander of the devil. In a very subtle way the serpent in the garden of Eden represented God to Eve as One who did not really care for her or her husband. As Satan continuously works against us—so we must put on "the girdle of God's truth."

The breast-plate of righteousness. *Form of attack—evil and sinful desires.* If Satan cannot pierce our armour by lies, he will try evil. He will bombard our minds with evil thoughts; he will try to influence our motives and sway our wills. The answer to this is God's righteousness, not our own! How many have tried to ward off these blows with the flimsy armour of their own goodness. Satan's arrows pierce it immediately. But, if we are Christians, we have God's righteousness to defend ourselves with. Then let us wear it like a piece of armour. Evil thoughts are not sin until they are entertained. They are like the gate-crashers at a party; we can accept them and let them stay, or firmly show them where the door is. That is what we must do when Satan attacks us with evil—show Satan the door. That is enough. Satan cannot pierce the armour of God's righteousness. He may bruise us, but he cannot wound us.

The sandals of the gospel of peace. *Form of attack—an easy and lazy life.* If Satan cannot disturb us, then he will try to make us as comfortable and cosy as possible—so that we won't disturb him! He will stop his attacks and sue for peace, but on completely unacceptable terms for a Christian. "Leave me alone," he will say, "and I will leave you alone." We dare not parley with Satan. The early Christians would not have been persecuted had they stopped their evangelism. But they suffered at the hands of the Jewish authorities because they refused to do so.

It is all too easy to fall for this subtle attack of the enemy, and go along with "carpet slipper Christianity." Some today are "at ease in Zion," journeying to heaven in first-class comfort. Satan has seen to it that such Christians have laid down their arms and are no longer concerned to attack and invade enemy-held territory.

The answer to this form of temptation is to get our shoes on, leave the comforts of home, and go out after those who are Satan's captives. This is probably what Paul means here. Ronald Knox translates these words, "in readiness to publish the gospel." And it is the gospel of peace—for the only real peace that can be found in this world is through surrender to Christ, who is the Prince of Peace. And this is what the devil will do all in his power to stop. We need to remember that Jesus showed us that God's love is so great that He will always leave 99 per cent of the flock to rescue the 1 per cent. Should we not leave the 1 per cent to rescue the 99 per cent?

The shield of faith. *Form of attack—unbelief.* Paul himself wants his readers to be especially careful to have this protection. *"Above all,"* he writes. For unbelief in its various guises is the most formidable kind of attack, and the shield of faith is the most important part of the gospel armour. The tense of the verb implies a constant and unflinching attitude of faith. Martin Luther knew this vicious form of attack on many occasions, and knew that the only protection was through faith in the promises of God. He writes somewhere out of deep conviction:

> The soul that clings to the promises of God with a firm faith is so united with them, altogether taken up into them, that it not only shares in all their power, but is saturated and made drunk with it . . . If a touch of Christ healed, how much more will this tender touch of the Spirit, this absorbing of the word, communicate to the soul all things that are the world's.

This is where our faith needs to be placed—firmly in the promises of God. In the epistle to the Hebrews the writer refers to the sin which "clings so closely." It is very likely from the context that the writer has in mind the sin of unbelief, for the previous chapter is taken up with the theme of faith and the great men and women who so truly exemplified it. Christians are to "lay aside" this besetting sin. No wonder Paul describes these attacks as "flaming darts." We all know what it is to be wounded by these fearful weapons of Satan. We know the doubts that assail us, and the fear of failure that cripples action.

"Is God really hearing me?" "Has He forgotten me?" "Has it worked?" "Will it last?" and so on. Easy, isn't it, to have 90 per cent faith and only 10 per cent doubt!

An excellent example of the word of God being spoken aloud, and so bringing someone to faith, may be seen in the life of Barclay Buxton. During his missionary work in Japan he was attacked by fear in this way. So he said repeatedly aloud the words from Hebrews 13:5-6, "he has said, 'I will never fail you nor forsake you.' Hence we can confidently say, 'The Lord is my helper, I will not be afraid; what can man do to me?' " He said these words until by faith he had made them his own, and so can we.

The only answer is the shield of faith. And remember this is not our puny faith, but God's strong faith. Paul calls it "the faith of the son of God" in Galatians 2:20. We are holding up the faith of Christ between ourselves and those fiery darts. Such faith is inpenetrable armour. The shield that Paul is probably thinking of here was the one the Roman legions carried into battle. It covered them from head to foot—but not their backs. There was no allowance made for deserters, says Corrie ten Boom.

The helmet of salvation. *Form of attack—calamity and accident.* The word salvation (*soteris*) is used in the New Testament to describe physical as well as spiritual well-being. For instance, it is used to describe the strength gained from eating in Acts 27:34, when Paul urged the sailors to have a meal before their ship came ashore on the island of Malta. In

Hebrews 11:7 it is used to describe how Noah and his family were saved from drowning in the flood. According to Souter it was commonly used of "deliverance from every calamity, and victory over enemies."

Satan will not stop at anything to destroy the work of God. He will make Christians ill. How often we read in the Journals of John Wesley how nausea and faintness came upon that great man before he was to preach. But he would carry on, sometimes barely able to climb the steps of the pulpit. But the moment he began to speak, the sickness would pass away. The enemy was defeated in his attempt to prevent the gospel from being preached. How often Christians languish ill in bed, when they should be resisting the devil's attacks and about their master's business!

Satan will sometimes try to kill God's servants. Jesus said of him, "he was a murderer from the beginning" (John 8:44). He tried to kill Jesus on several occasions before the divinely appointed time for that death. Once He was miraculously saved from mob violence, and on another occasion from drowning in the lake of Galilee. But Jesus survived in order to finish the work that the Father had sent Him to do. And we should expect the same protection until the moment comes when we can echo the words of Jesus, "I have finished the work which you gave me to do."

Of course there will be times when God allows death by violence. There was the case of Stephen, the first Christian martyr, whose career seemed to be so full of promise. Satan must have been glad to see him removed so quickly from the scene of his triumphs. But little did he realise that standing by was Saul of Tarsus, who was so obviously deeply affected by what he saw of the sufferings of Stephen, and who was before long to become an even more effective evangelist. But we need to beware of the attacks of Satan. The roads, for instance, are becoming increasingly dangerous. We should always pray before setting out, claiming the protection of the name of Jesus—and also that our driving will be skilful and unselfish. So let us put on the "crash-helmet" of salvation as well as our seat-belts.

The Name of Jesus

We have already seen in the chapter "Our Weapons" how Christ's name is a real power in spiritual warfare. We noticed that the name of a person in the Bible means the entire person. When, therefore, we talk about the protection of the name of Jesus, we do not mean that there is something magical about the word and that it is protective in itself. No, the name of Jesus means the protective power of His presence and all that He is today because of all that He did on the Cross. As Proverbs expresses it, "the name of the Lord is a strong tower; the righteous man runs into it and is safe" (18:10).

This form of protection was bequeathed to us by our Lord when He prayed for the Church before He went into the garden of Gethsemane. "Holy Father, protect by the power of thy name those whom thou hast given me, that they may be one, as we are one. When I was with them, I protected by the power of thy name those whom thou hast given me, and kept them safe" (John 17:11-12 NEB). And our Lord still keeps us safe through his powerful name.

There are some who regard the blood of Christ as protective. But in the Bible the blood always answers to the guilt of sin—that is why it is always Godward. The two scriptures which some use as the basis for the protective nature of the blood also bear this out. In the story of the escape from Egypt, the blood which was daubed on the door-posts and lintels of the Israelites was for God to see, not the devil! "I will pass over you," says God (Exod. 12:13). The other reference is Revelation 12:11. "They conquered him [Satan] by the blood of the Lamb and by the word of their testimony." Here Satan appears in the context as "the accuser of the brethren." The blood, therefore, in this verse is protective against guilt.

The value of the name of Jesus is that it combines the efficacy of his death with his resurrection life. It means "Saviour"—and refers to One who is alive for ever and raised "far above all." It is the living Christ who protects his people—standing by them and working with them. But it is Christ who shed his blood and died on the Cross. Without the shedding of blood there would have been no remission of sins or power over Satan. In this sense, the blood of Christ is an indispensable part of our salvation and, *therefore,* of our protection.

The Angelic Hosts

In the general scepticism within the Church today, in which the supernatural has been debunked, the presence and value of angels is seldom if ever recognised. Like the servant of the prophet Elisha, we need to have our eyes opened to the protective ring of angels, which is at all times around God's people. As the Psalmist says, "the angel of the Lord encamps around those who fear Him, and delivers them" (34:7).

In the Acts of the Apostles angels seem to be as much in evidence as their satanic counterparts, the evil spirits. They seem to be specialists in jail-breaking, for twice they manage to get the apostles and Peter out of prison. They also helped in directing God's plans in evangelism. It was an angel, for example, who directed Philip to the desert of Gaza to contact the Ethiopian eunuch. When Paul was in danger of losing his life in a storm at sea, it was an angel that reassured him. If the demonic powers have not given up the struggle and returned to hell since New Testament days, are we to imagine that the angels are less powerfully present than they were in the days of the apostles of our Lord?

In the epistle to the Hebrews we are told about people who have "entertained angels unawares" (13:2). Much of our thinking about angels is conditioned by artists' impressions of them. One would not have thought there was much chance of modern man entertaining such angels (wings and all) without being aware of it! We may never know whether or not we have actually seen such angels, but the fact of their presence should be comforting. We are not to attempt to communicate with them, and should remember that Satan can disguise himself as an angel of light.

With God's protection, and wielding His weapons, we can enter confidently into warfare with Satan.

TEN

Battle Areas

L ET US CONSIDER the areas of our lives which are at times
fought over. It is important that we see clearly where the
enemy is likely to attack, so that we can not only prepare
defences, but also our forces to counter-attack and drive the
enemy away.

It is here that a major error is sometimes made, which leads to
faulty diagnosis and great harm to individuals. One is referring
to a type of dualism which is based on a faulty premise. Some
seem to assume that the whole world is either under the control
of God or Satan. Therefore, everything that happens can be
attributed either to a divine or satanic cause. With this kind of
thinking there can be no place for natural or human factors.
This has led some Christians to grossly exaggerated views of the
activity of evil spirits, so that all illnesses, including the
psychological, and all temptations are due to demonic forces.
Even natural weaknesses and infirmities, and the temptations
which, according to Paul, are "common to all men," are treated
as cases in need of exorcism. Confusion and personal damage
has been caused by such faulty diagnosis. For some people have
been led to expect release from the disciplines, hardships and
temptations of the Christian way of life. It would indeed be
comforting to the flesh to be set free from temptation and other
forms of spiritual conflict. But we will have to wait for death
before such a happy release takes place.

So many of the problems that face us have a perfectly
reasonable or "natural" explanation. Many are due to what Paul

calls "the flesh"—our self life. Paul tells us to "reckon ourselves dead unto sin," not to chase off to the nearest deliverance expert for a "release." There is no substitute for self-discipline in the Christian life, and the source of this should not be a slavish form of legalism, but the presence and power of the Holy Spirit, for the last but not least fruit of the Spirit is "self-control." However, we still have to exercise that discipline, through the power of the Spirit. In counselling one often finds that a perfectly natural explanation can be found for some disorder, and that what is really needed is a holiday, or a regular day of rest, or the discipline of fasting or some other form of self-denial. The real answer to our problem may be to humble ourselves and write some letters of apology. Too many today are getting tied to the apron-strings of counsellors, and may find themselves as a result in greater bondage than ever. Often the real antidote is the basic Christian principle of repentance, without which a harmonious relationship with God and people is impossible. When this is neglected people get themselves into impossible relationship tangles. We have to learn to confess our faults to one another and seek forgiveness where necessary. And even if we can attribute a large measure of our problem to Satan's power and activity, we are still responsible before God and need to repent. The neglect of this basic principle is a cause of spiritual disorders in the Church and amongst its individual members. Paul called it "not discerning the Body." He goes on, "that is why many of you are feeble and sick, and a number have died. But if we examine ourselves, we should not thus fall under judgement" (1 Cor. 11:30-31 NEB). Our warfare against Satan is no substitute for true repentance.

Now we must look at some of the battle areas.

The Physical

If our body is the temple of the Holy Spirit, then it will also be a target of Satan. Yet it is surprising today to find so many Christians who appear oblivious to this area of attack. Instead of resisting Satan, they "take it on the chin" without so much as a complaint, and allow him to deprive their bodies of strength and efficiency.

If Paul's "thorn in the flesh" was a physical ailment, and there are some who would argue otherwise, then he clearly regarded it as a satanic attack, "a messenger of Satan to harrass me," as he put it. The word "messenger" is normally translated "angel," and, as we have seen earlier, this sometimes refers to an evil spirit. Some people have strongly fixed in their minds that a person who is attacked by an evil spirit must be a very poor Christian. But here we are told that God allows Paul to be attacked to keep him from being too elated "by the abundance of revelations" (2 Cor. 12:7). It was because he had been so wonderfully blessed that this attack was allowed to come upon him.

In the gospels we are told that Jesus sometimes healed people by means of casting out an evil spirit. Thus He dealt with dumbness (Matt. 9:32-33), blindness (Matt. 12:22) and deafness (Mark 9:25). It is surely significant that the senses seem particularly prone to attack in the gospel narrative. The explanation surely is that it is through such senses, speech, sight and hearing, that the gospel is largely communicated. No wonder the enemy will particularly attack these vital organs of the body.

There was a minister who had been partially deaf for several years. His deafness came upon him when he was going through a really tough spiritual battle. He had received the laying on of hands, and although there was healing for a time, the deafness returned. However, when the deaf spirit was commanded to go in the name of Jesus, there was immediate healing and restoration of hearing so that he was able to dispense with his hearing aid permanently.

In the United States a young officer in the Salvation Army, who had been born blind, was brought to a meeting at which Mrs. Jean Darnall was ministering. A word of knowledge was given by the Holy Spirit revealing the cause of the blindness. This man had been born in prison. The father was a criminal and the mother had conspired with him. It is not to be wondered at that an evil spirit had been able to enter this baby at birth, causing the blindness. When the spirit had been cast out, the young man saw perfectly for the first time in his life.

Let it be emphasised that not all illness is caused in this way. Many attacks on our bodies are satanic rather than specifically demonic. Some illness is caused by sin, though not always the sin of the sick person. We will need the gifts of the Spirit to discern the basis of the illness before we can pray for the person in need. It is very important that the counselling and prayer should be conducted with a truly compassionate spirit. Far more illness is caused by the sin of others than is often realised.

The Moral

This is a much more obvious and well-known area of attack. Satan will from time to time tempt us to break God's moral laws, and so bring dishonour on the name of his Son. Every Christian knows what this means, and we have to fight a continual battle against the enemy, who is unremitting and at times ferocious in his attacks upon us. But "God is faithful," as Paul puts it, "he will not let you be tempted beyond your strength, but with the temptation will also provide the way of escape, that you may be able to endure it" (1 Cor. 10:13).

But there are times when these temptations become compulsions. It seems that the enemy is able to form a bridgehead—and all efforts seem futile. The person is in bondage to some habit of thought or action, and knows it. No amount of resisting will budge the enemy—he is in occupation. We are not to "give place to the devil," and there may have been failure here, or there may be some other factor which has allowed Satan this strong position.

Let us give some examples of what we mean. There is the temptation to steal, common to all at times, but there is also a compulsion to steal called kleptomania, which is usually completely irrational. We hear of comparatively wealthy people caught stealing small items of grocery from a supermarket. Or there is the temptation to sexual misconduct, again common to all at times, but there can be a compulsive form of lust, again irrational, for the person is often happily married, yet is driven to fall into sin. No amount of praying, fasting or self-discipline seems to have any effect. In such cases the person may well need the ministry of another for deliverance from such a bondage, or in extreme cases from an evil spirit.

There are a variety of forms of bondage in this category— chain smoking, compulsive gambling, sexual perversions, extreme hatred or a murderous spirit, alcoholism, lying, drug addiction, sadism, indecent exposure, a violent temper, blaspheming and swearing, covetousness that leads to exorbitant spending, and so on. It is important that we do not imagine that all such bondages are the work of evil spirits. But we should be open to the possibility.

A young married woman came to a conference a compulsive chain smoker. Feeling guilty about this habit, she would find some private place to satisfy this craving for a cigarette. Knowing of others who had been set free from similar habits she sought the help of Christians who in prayer released her from this hold of the enemy. Although strongly tempted to smoke again to begin with, she found "the way of escape" this time, and gradually the craving disappeared. She has never smoked since.

The Theological

Since the great design of Satan is to "deceive the nations," demonic powers are bound to be active in the theological field. This is a happy hunting ground for Satan, for one least expects to find a demon in the respectable confines of a theological college or the intellectual cut and thrust of refined theological debate! And those who are dominated by purely rational considerations will not readily accept, let alone attempt to deal with, such irrational notions as demonised theological opinions.

But it may well be that many of the destructive heresies of the past as well as the present were not the inventions of man at all, but the product of demonic influences. This was the view of

Paul, who warned that "in later times some will fall away from the faith, giving heed to seducing spirits and doctrines of demons" (1 Tim. 4:1). Paul envisages teaching being introduced at the instigation of evil spirits. Moreover, Satan is described by John as "the spirit of error" in contrast to the Holy Spirit, who is "the Spirit of truth." James does the same thing when he says that some so-called wisdom is "earthbound, sensual, *demonic* " (James 3:15 NEB).

John writes about this, "Beloved do not believe every spirit, but test the spirits to see whether they are of God; for many false prophets have gone out into the world. By this you know the Spirit of God: every spirit which confesses that Jesus Christ has come in the flesh is of God, and every spirit which does not confess Jesus is not of God" (John 4:1-3). This text has sometimes been misunderstood. It does not mean we are to test "spirits," *but rather to test teachers.* From statements made in the gospels the evil spirits seem to be more orthodox in their beliefs than many modern theologians! John means that we are to test the inspiration of the teachers.

In this cult-ridden world it is not hard to see why Satan has garnered such a fruitful harvest amongst the gullible and those, weakened by pride and vanity, who are open to temptation to seek for superior knowledge and new truth. Commenting on the widespread disharmony amongst Christians today, Merrill F. Unger writes:[16]

> Satan has thus gained a large advantage over many, because of a widely prevailing incomprehension of even the first principles of biblical demonology, and because of a manifest unacquaintance with even an elementary knowledge of the power and reality of demonic deception.

> Some of the modern cults can be directly traceable to occult and spiritistic origins. Their basis is very often a claim to some "higher revelation" which has come in some supernatural way. So people, instead of following the old and safe paths, have been side-tracked, lured away by fantastic illusions.

What follows from this is that we need to look at error and heresy sometimes from a new angle. We cannot regard it solely as a battle for the mind. We are not simply to try and convince people intellectually of the error of their teaching. Here too we are involved in spiritual warfare, and this requires spiritual weapons if men and women are to be delivered from the power of such "doctrines of demons."

Under this heading we should also mention fanaticism. Every revival seems to suffer from its ration of religious fanatics, who in their pride and folly jump on the band-wagon and bring division and confusion to some. Our own day, unfortunately, is not without their presence and influence.

In James 3:17 divine wisdom is defined as "first pure, then peaceable, gentle, open to reason, full of mercy and good fruits, without uncertainty or insincerity." A fanatical spirit, which comes from the enemy, is full of enthusiasm and energy, but the character of those who have such a spirit is closed to reason, harsh, dogmatic and cocksure. Such people are unwilling to listen to others, for they are so convinced that they are hearing the voice of God, any contrary opinion cannot be of God. They believe they are never wrong, but they bring, as James says, "disorder and every vile practice." Fanaticism causes more harm to God's cause than persecution, as John Wesley discovered. Persecution refines and purifies the Church, but fanaticism defiles it.

The Psychological

Man will often attribute what he does not understand to "psychological" factors. John Wesley once wrote about this: "when doctors meet with disorders which they do not understand, they commonly term them 'nervous,' a word that conveys to us no determinate idea, but it is a good cover for learned ignorance."

Today there is an increasing proportion of treatment which delves into a person's past in order to try to discover what lies behind irrational fears and complexes. In this field we need to tread carefully. There is a good deal of truth in what psychology has discovered. But the Christian can also have access to this realm and see results which are barred the unbelieving psychologist. But great care needs to be exercised.

Fear is one of the commonest elements in psychological illness, and it is significantly called "a spirit of fear" by Paul, and contrasted with the Holy Spirit (2 Tim. 1:7). In Hebrews 2:15 the ultimate fear, that of death, is described as a form of bondage. This does indicate that fear, so often irrational, can be dealt with in the spiritual realm rather than the purely rational.

This complex subject needs a far more detailed examination than is possible here. But it should be emphasised that it ill betides anyone to attribute all factors in this area to evil sources. It would be an over-simplification. On the other hand, it is equally wrong to dismiss satanic influences from this area, as if they play no part. A careful diagnosis is all important, and sometimes healing does follow an exorcism. The obvious psychological illness to relate to demonic activity is schizophrenia, where there are two apparently quite separate parts to a person's life. One has known healing come from an exorcism in this field, but one has also known well-documented cases where healing has come from another source of treatment.

Here, then, are two cases which illustrate how the enemy sometimes operates in this area. A mature Christian man revealed privately that he had been subjected all his life to irrational nightmares. It also affected his Christian life, and there seemed to be a lack of freedom in worship and witness. It was disclosed that as a small boy he had lived with his parents in a house that was shared by a spiritualist family. One day this boy's mother discovered the whole family dead. The father had murdered his wife and children and then taken his own life. The shock was transmitted to the son. After this had been revealed the man was prayed for and set free from a spirit of fear. He experienced immediate release and freedom, and the nightmares ceased.

A young woman experienced serious psychological harm when still a baby through the most distressing circumstances.

Her long search for love provided soil for Satan to bring her life into serious bondage and disorders of various kinds—physical, moral and psychological. It was accompanied by a crippling fear and guilt. After exorcism there was an overwhelming sense of grief, which proved a means of healing, for the love of God was then able to be poured into her heart which overflowed in praise and release in the gift of speaking in tongues. The psychiatrist who had been attending her saw his first proof that divine healing of very early psychological damage is possible.

The Psychical

We have already seen in a previous chapter how the Church's early contact with alien spiritual forces demanded strong action and many exorcisms. We have also seen that in the spiritual realm there are no neutral forces. The spirits of the dead are forbidden to communicate with us, and we with them. The case of the slave girl in Acts 16 is an interesting one, for she obviously possessed an unusual gift of discernment, albeit from an evil source. She spoke words that were true—in fact, she provided the apostles with a free publicity service—"these men are servants of the most high God," she cried, "who proclaim to you the way of salvation." But she was drawing people's attention to men rather than to Christ, and this may have been one of the factors that convinced Paul that this woman had an evil spirit. But it is vital to notice that there is no suggestion that this power of divination should be "taken over" and converted to working for Christ rather than Satan and her employers. It is cast out of the woman.

The experience of a certain woman is an illustration of this point. She had a quite uncanny gift of perception far beyond what we sometimes call "feminine intuition." She knew when accidents were going to happen, and very useful information such as where the cheapest vegetables were being sold! This was discerned as a spirit of divination, and through prayer she was fully delivered from it. But in its place she now has a deeper discernment through the Holy Spirit, which promises to develop into a healthy and edifying ministry to others.

Numerous examples could be given of the way in which Satan has interfered with the lives of Christians, bringing them into bondage through spiritualistic contacts. Dr. Kurt Koch's book *Between Christ and Satan,* the result of extensive research and counselling over many years, shows conclusively that this is so. In fact, the link is so common that always in counselling an invariable question to anyone with a spiritual disorder, such as real difficulties in praying, depression, lack of inclination to read the Bible or enter into fellowship, should be—"have you ever had any contact with spiritualism or any other form of divination?"

The Church in certain quarters has opened its doors to spiritualism and unwittingly let satanic powers loose, with disastrous results. In the early days of the Church no compromise was permitted with other religious practices. It was most disturbing to see in New Zealand, for instance, Maori churches decorated with the symbols of their old religion. But such has been the spirit of compromise in the Church for more than a century.

Children

A very important aspect of this subject is the degree to which children can be attacked by Satan and his evil spirits. In the New Testament there are cases. There is a boy mentioned (Mark 9:14-29) and a girl (Matt. 15:22). In the latter case the healing took place at a distance, for Jesus never actually visited the woman's daughter. As we have seen the ancient baptismal liturgies in the Western Church allowed for exorcisms, and this was kept in the Prayer Book of 1549, although subsequently dropped.

Children are particularly vulnerable to all kinds of experiences and pressures. There is no reason to think that they are free from enemy attacks; in fact, in many ways they are more open and need very much the protection of the believing prayers of their parents.

In conversation one night with a minister and his wife it was discovered that they had problems with their two children. One displayed the most peculiar and irrational behaviour at times, behaving more like an animal than a child. He also displayed healing powers, something unusual in such a young person. Their other son was unable to speak, although then well past the normal age when children begin to talk. The parents were naturally very worried about this. After questioning it was discovered that in a previous church appointment they had occupied a house which had for many years been the home of a minister who practised spiritualism openly and unashamedly. One of these sons had been born there, and the other had been living there during his most impressionable years. The evil influence of the house had been felt by the villagers as well as this family. After these facts had been established the boys were prayed over while they were still sleeping, and the power of Satan cut off from them. Within a few days the younger son was speaking, and the first word he spoke was "Jesus," while with the other son there was never again a recurrence of the peculiar behaviour which had caused the parents such anxiety.

You will notice that prayer was made while the children were asleep. This is possible with young children, who, as in this case, are the innocent victims of the sins of others. In fact, audible prayer and reassuring words, especially the word of God itself, can reach and bring blessing to people in sleep. Children, for example, who suffer from nightmares can experience healing of the memories through this kind of therapy, as long as, of course, it is ministered through the Holy Spirit.

In our ministry to children we have to be very careful not to bring fear to them, and if we pray for them audibly when they are conscious, then we should explain simply what we are going to do, and frame it in language which will not scare them, but rather comfort and reassure them. Taught properly, young children have a surprisingly mature grasp and appreciation of spiritual truth, and will at a very tender age understand the nature of spiritual warfare. They can profitably be shown how to recognise and overcome the attacks of Satan without fear.

Should we really be surprised at all this, when we remember that Jesus said "of such is the Kingdom of God"?

Places

If God manifests His presence in places, as He did so gloriously in the temple in the Old Testament and at Pentecost in the New, so that we are told that the Holy Spirit "filled all the house where they were sitting," it is equally true that satanic power can infiltrate buildings and rooms and create an unholy and disturbing influence. Churches, as one would expect, are especially a battle area. We all know church buildings in which the presence of God is immediately felt, whereas there are others which seem to have another atmosphere, and this is not the fault of the architecture or furnishings, tempted though we may be to blame them. And the same is true of houses.

In 1967 I experienced during the night feelings of gloom and fear, particularly of death, which were unusual for me. At first I thought it might have something to do with my personal life. After a time the fears were worse, and I became convinced that there was something unpleasant about the house itself. We had only just moved in, and it was quite an old building. A man who was especially sensitive to the spiritual realm felt the same when he came and stayed with us. With the Bishop's permission, Dom Robert Petitpierre, an Anglican Benedictine monk, who had wide experience of such matters, came and stayed the night with us. He conducted a Communion service in the house and exorcised every room according to the form which can be found in the appendix (p. 106). From that day onwards the atmosphere in the house changed and there was no recurrence of the experience which I have related. We need to claim buildings as well as people for the Lordship of Christ.

In order to clarify the situation we have divided the "battle-field" into certain areas. In practice it is almost impossible to classify the conflict into such water-tight compartments. Man is a whole being composed of many parts, and each part inter-acts with the others. So a truly accurate assessment of the battle situation may have to take into account a number of these areas together. Thus the moral may affect the physical, and so on. But the Holy Spirit, who leads us into all truth, will guide us and give us discernment as we minister to one another and help each other to fight the "good fight of the faith."

ELEVEN

Defeating the Enemy

W E HAVE BEEN LOOKING at the areas of our life which may come under the attacks of Satan. In this chapter we shall see the ways of resisting and defeating the enemy, and delivering these areas from his control and influence. But before we do this we should consider *how* the enemy attacks and what his tactics are. For our own tactics will depend very largely on the mode of attack.

Basically, there are three forms of attack, and these can be likened in military terms to:

(a) a frontal assault (or from the flank)
(b) a siege or blockade
(c) an invasion and occupation.

The common experiences of temptation, whether they come directly or indirectly (i.e., from the flank), are like the straightforward assault. They may be brief, after which the enemy retreats, or sustained pressure, which some call an oppression. A "bondage" is like the siege or blockade, where the enemy breaks through and surrounds an area. For with a bondage, a part of our life is brought under the enemy's control. The enemy does not possess the area, but he can prevent it from functioning properly, and his tactics are to cut it off from the rest of the area which is in our hands. The third is where the enemy actually occupies a part of our life. It is no longer under our control at all.

There are obvious limitations to these illustrations, but they may help to give us a rough idea of what the enemy is up to, and the extent of the damage he can do in our lives. The first kind of attack is, of course, commonly experienced by every Christian, and the way to deal with it is resistance. "Resist the devil, and he will flee from you." In the case of the sustained kind of attack, the resistance too needs to be kept up, aided if at all possible by the help of other Christians who understand what is happening.

The second kind of attack is less common. A bondage is some habit or way of life or wrong relationship which has got a hold on a person, and even a firm resistance is insufficient to shake him free from it. The way to deal with it is loosing; this normally has to be done by another Christian, who thereby "raises the siege" or helps to "relieve the blockade."

The third kind of attack or influence is even less common. Here the person is completely under the control of an evil spirit in some area of his or her life. The way to deal with it is casting out. This has to be done by other Christians who take authority over the enemy, and so oust him from his position of occupation, freeing the person to serve God.

The boundary line between these three is not always clearly defined, but discernment will be given and discretion as to how to act.

One of the major questions that arises from this is whether or not a Christian can be "possessed" by an evil spirit. Quite a lot has been written and said about this matter, but the whole question is affected by what we mean by "possession." It may have been noticed that the word has been deliberately avoided in this book. The reason for this is important. The fault here lies with the Bible translators, because they have used the word "possession," which is not a strict rendering of the Greek. In fact the Bible never talks about a person being "possessed." The Greek refers to people either "having" an evil spirit, or being "demonised" (*daimonizomai*). Possession suggests a complete take-over of the person, which is not necessarily the case with one who has an evil spirit. In the gospels there were some, like the Gadarene demoniac, who were obviously mentally deranged and today would be certified in-patients of a mental hospital.

But there were others who were normal members of society, attending the synagogue for worship and otherwise accepted within the community. So today there are cases of demonisation which are quite as extreme as the demoniacs in the gospels, but many others which are not immediately discernible.

To sum up, if by "possession" we mean the complete "take-over" of the personality so that it comes entirely under the control of Satan, then we can say without hesitation that no true Christian can experience such a thing. But this is not what is being described in the New Testament. In the sense of "having" an evil spirit, then no Christian is immune. As we have seen in some of the cases cited, some Christians have had these spirits before they became Christians. It is true that many are set free from them when they believe or are baptised. But many retain them because there is no one to minister to them and bring deliverance. Perhaps the Church of England and other churches should not so quickly have abandoned exorcism in the service of baptism, for it is the time of Christian initiation which is the most appropriate for such ministry. It needs to be added that it is equally possible to be baptised or filled with the Holy Spirit and not be released from satanic bondages. In recent years this fact has been confirmed again and again in personal ministry. But now we should consider in detail how we should proceed with the ministry.

Our Preparation

There is a need for genuine love and a gentle spirit in helping others in this way. We can get rough with Satan, but not with those who have become his victims. There is no need for noise. Satan and his angels will not be frightened off by this. But they will go as soon as the word of authority is spoken in faith.

We should never go lightly into this ministry. First, we should seek personal cleansing, in the same way as a surgeon will wash before an operation. We should repent of any sin, and relinquish any trust or confidence in ourselves. We must confess, if necessary, any unbelief in the power of our Lord and the authority of his word.

We should then put on the armour of God, piece by piece, leaving nothing to chance. You can pray something like this:

Heavenly Father
I claim by faith now the protection of your armour, that I may stand against Satan and all his hosts, and in the name of Jesus overcome them.
I take your truth to counter the lies and errors of a cunning enemy.
I take your righteousness to overcome the evil thoughts and accusations of Satan.
I take the equipment of the gospel of peace and forsake the safety and comforts of life in order to wage war with the enemy.
Above all, I take your faith to bar the way to doubts and unbelief entering my soul.
I take your salvation, and trust you to protect my body and soul from Satan's varied attacks.
I take your word, and pray that the Holy Spirit will enable me to use it effectively against the enemy and to sever every bondage and deliver every captive of Satan.
In the strong and all-conquering name of Jesus Christ, my Lord.
Amen.

Paul goes on in this passage to refer to "praying in the Holy Spirit." At this point, and before praying for the person in need, it is advisable to pray for a time in tongues, if one has received this gift. It will edify us for the work that lies ahead. Paul also cautions, "keep alert with all perseverance." This we must continue to do.

The Ministry

Repentance. However powerless we are in the face of satanic onslaughts, sin should always be recognised, confessed and forsaken. Of course, one would like to say, "you could not help it," or "it was not your fault." But there can be no full deliverance, where a person's sin is a major factor, unless there is a frank recognition of it and a willingness with the help of God's grace to give it up. This is not easy. When sin is indulged in repeatedly, there is a dulling of conscience and conviction. One is tempted to allow excuses. Lovingly but firmly, for the sake of the person concerned, there should be an insistence on this repentance.

The person may have been more sinned against than sinning. In that case the temptation will often be to store up resentment and bitterness. If this has been done, then it will need to be confessed also.

Some Anglicans, and of course Roman Catholics, are used to making their confession to a minister or a priest. Every person we minister to should be made aware of God's love, the joy of forgiveness, reconciliation, and restoration. God understands us and is never shocked at our confession. He knows all about it. It is only the proud, the unreal and the insincere that He refuses. We need to bind up the spiritual wounds of repentance and pour into them the full measure of God's free pardon through the Cross of his Son, and his unrelenting love. We will need to read together the word of God, explaining as simply as we know how the meaning of the Cross and the power of the blood to cleanse. Perhaps we shall look at verses like 1 Timothy 1:15 or 1 John 1:5-10 and so on. We should persist until we are sure that forgiveness has really been accepted and the way of God has been believed.

Deliverance. Now has come the time for setting the prisoner free. It is glorious to know of the power and authority given to *us* to do this. We must remember that we do not ask God to resist the devil or to loose the captive; God has told us to do this, and has given us the authority to do it in the name of his Son. So this is not a prayer to God, but a command to Satan to flee or to give up the captive he has bound. The words we use at this stage will vary according to the circumstances, and there is no set formula. Here Christian practice is very different from pagan, for it is not the words themselves that are important, so much as the faith and authority with which we say them.

1. Resisting—In this chapter we are particularly concerned with the question of our ministry to others. Obviously in the daily warfare we face and the constant experiences of temptation, we do not have to go through a lengthy procedure like this, or need the help of another Christian. Perhaps many times a day we shall have to "resist the devil"—and he will flee. But here we are concerned with deeper problems and needs. All of us find that there are times when something tries to get on top of us—when we have a tougher battle than usual. We may get really run down and depressed. Of course we should not always be running to another Christian for help. But there is the exception. We can pray together with someone, and our friend's faith and authority help to buttress our own. Often the oppression will lift and we will be able to rejoice together. This is part of the blessing of being members of the Body of Christ; we are able to "bear one another's burdens, and so fulfil the law of Christ" (Gal. 6:2).

2. Binding and loosing—Jesus told his disciples when teaching them about this kind of ministry, "first bind the strong man" (Matt. 12:29). The picture our Lord paints is of a powerful Eastern potentate and the need to "plunder his house." If a burglar wants to break and enter a house, then he must first make sure that the occupants are neutralised. A strong person is not going to sit around watching his house being broken into and his possessions stolen. Neither is Satan going to let us into his kingdom without putting up very strong resistance. The enemy must first be neutralised before we can release his captives.

So in prayer we bind Satan. Notice *we do it* —we do not ask our Lord to. We may say something like this:

In Jesus' name, I (or we if more than one are ministering) bind you, Satan, that you no longer exercise dominion over this person.

In speaking about the Church, Jesus gave us this promise: "whatever you bind on earth shall be bound in heaven, and whatever you loose on earth shall be loosed in heaven" (Matt. 16:19). This is repeated by our Lord in Matthew 18:18. The trouble with this verse is that so many Protestants have spent their energies seeking to prove that this does not refer to the Pope, or to priestly absolution, that they have largely neglected to find out what it does refer to! Likewise Roman Catholics have so ardently defended their position that they too seem to have restricted and misapplied it. Surely amongst other things it is another reference to our authority to bind evil powers in Jesus' name and to loose those who are subjected to bondage. And even if the Matthew 16 reference could be said to refer to Peter (and to his successors, as Roman Catholics would say), it is a plural "you" in Matthew 18, and so refers to any member of the Body of Christ, for the context makes it clear that in the local church situation the power and authority to bind and loose is to be exercised quite apart from an "apostle" being present.

Having, therefore, bound Satan, we have to set free his captives. Yes, *we* have the authority to do this, and we do not ask our Lord to. Here is a suggested prayer which Mrs. Anne White uses:

> In the name of Jesus, by the power of his precious blood shed on the Cross for you personally, I take the sword of the Spirit and cut you free from bondage to (and here one names the particular bondage).

When Jesus raised Lazarus from the dead, he came out of the grave with "his hands and feet bound with bandages, and his face wrapped with a cloth" (John 11:44). Jesus said to those who were with him, "unbind him and let him go." Jesus raised Lazarus from the dead, but He asked others to loose him from the grave clothes. This is a good illustration of this ministry, for there are Christians who certainly have new life in Christ. He has raised them from spiritual death. But they are still bound by some of the habits and tendencies of the old life. They can scarcely shuffle along, let alone walk naturally and freely. It is for us to loose them and let them go free. There are others whose lives are crippled by irrational fears and complexes. But Jesus came to set us free from these things.

3. *Casting out*—Just as we have avoided the word "possession," so too we have tried not to use the word "exorcism." It is impossible to avoid it altogether, as it is the word which is in current use. But it was never actually used in the Bible, where the word employed is "cast out" (*ekballo*), rather than *exorkizo*. Merrill F. Unger writes about this:[17]

> Strictly speaking there are no exorcisms in the Bible. Use of the word, in its essential etymological meaning, forbids its employment with regard to the expulsion of demons by our Lord or his disciples. The word signifying, as it does, the casting out of evil spirits by conjurations, incantations, or religious or magical ceremonies, is singularly appropriate to describe Jewish and ethnic practice, but is in salient contrast to that of our Lord and his followers, who employed no such methods. Among ancient and primitive peoples, exorcism depended to a great extent on the efficacy of magical formulas . . . Power to cast out demons was regarded as existing in the words themselves, and great importance was attached to the correct recital of the right formulas and proper performance of the prescribed ritual.

To bind and to loose is one thing, but to cast out is another. The one as we have seen, is like raising a siege; the other is like evicting an army of occupation. The one needs to be loosed, but the person with an evil spirit needs to have it cast out.

The name or nature of the evil spirit will probably have been revealed to us, for, as we have seen, they usually affect a person in a particular area of life or a part of the body. In this case we name the spirit when we command it to leave the person. The practice that some follow of asking the demons for their names has no scriptural warrant. There is no instance of Jesus doing it;

in Mark 5 he asked the *man* what his name was, and it is the man who answers, "my name is legion," although the demons may have added the words "for we are many" (Mark 5:9). As for carrying on a conversation with them, this is extremely dangerous and scripturally unwarranted. Jesus commanded them to be silent, for although they knew the truth all right, they were not good witnesses to it! One has even heard of people tape-recording these sessions. Evil is not something to be "examined" or recorded for posterity. To be curious in this way is to invite Satan to trap the very ones who are seeking to be deliverers. In Acts 19 Paul saw to it that everything to do with the evil which had been practised in Ephesus was burnt, even though it was extremely valuable. In the previous section we mentioned the matter of binding Satan. This, of course, applies also to casting out. If we need to "bind the strong man" before loosing someone, we shall certainly need to bind his spirits before casting them out, so that they do not hurt or upset the person as they leave.

In the appendix there are a number of forms of exorcism which have been used in the Church for centuries. Simplicity should be the order of the day. Here is a suggestion:

In the name of Jesus Christ I/we command you evil spirit (here the spirit is named) to come out of this person and never enter him/her again.

The laying on of hands is inappropriate for the actual casting out, but should be used in the subsequent ministry of strengthening by the in-filling of the Holy Spirit, and healing the delivered person from any damage which may have been done by demonic forces.

A struggle may take place in extreme cases. Sometimes the spirits refuse to come out immediately, and a protracted battle has been known to take place. But this should not normally happen. Jesus certainly did not waste valuable time on these evil powers, and there is no need for us to burn the midnight oil in seeking a person's deliverance. If freedom does not come at once, it is probably an indication either that we need more preparation and discernment ourselves, and this may involve us in a time of prayer and fasting, or that the person is not quite ready or willing to be delivered, and the hour of full deliverance has not yet come. It may also be that we are the wrong persons involved in the ministry. Failure is never in the authority given to us in the name of Jesus. Sometimes these long sessions of casting out are part of the enemy's plan to tire out Christian people, while at other times, it is the person himself who is clamouring for attention of the wrong sort, or even notoriety. Of course, if our diagnosis has been wrong in the first place, and there is no evil spirit involved, then no wonder there will be nothing to show for it.

There is no need for shouting and screaming. If there are manifestations, then they will come of their own accord and should never be suggested to the person being prayed for. In the gospels evil spirits did come out "screaming," and we should be ready for this eventuality. But there were other times when was no recorded manifestation. There is, these days, too much for manifestations when a spirit leaves a person (coughing, weeping, etc.), whereas the initial manifestation revealing the presence of an evil spirit, perhaps during a talk or prayer, is far important. They often anyway leave a person very quietly, especially if the spirits have been bound, as already mentioned.

When an evil spirit comes out of a person, it will want to go somewhere else, although it is not altogether a free agent, for in Mark 5 the spirits had to ask permission to go into the pigs. Jesus described them as "walking through waterless places seeking rest" (Matt. 12:43). Restlessness is often a feature of the satanic. In Job Satan describes his activity as "going to and fro on the earth, and from walking up and down on it" (Job 1:7). He is pictured too in 1 Peter as a restless lion (5:8). The demons are the same. Jesus also warns us that they may gang up with several other worse spirits and try to force a re-entry into the life of the person delivered. It may have been noticed in the suggested wording of the casting out that there was a command "never to enter again." This is what Jesus said in **Mark 9:25.** But beyond this we cannot go. We only have a mandate to cast spirits out, not to tell them where to go. None of the ancient rites of exorcism tell the evil spirit where to go. There are some people who tell the evil spirits to go to the lake of fire or hell. But as this will not take place until the day of judgement, the only thing we can do is to hand them over to the sovereign power and authority of the Lord himself.

I command you to go where the Lord Jesus Christ sends you, and never to return to this person. I place you under the authority of Him who is "far above all."

After-care

1. Filling—Jesus tells us in the gospels that there is a vacuum caused by the exit of evil spirits (Matt. 12:44). The house is "empty, swept and put in order." There is what we call today "vacant possession." Indeed our Lord has done such a thorough springclean that it is invitingly ready for re-occupation. But by whom? We must see to it that the enemy finds the door locked and bolted when he returns, and the Lord himself in full possession of his servant. If the person we have ministered to has not received the baptism or fullness of the Holy Spirit, this may well be the right moment to tell him about it, and to pray with him. This is a time when people are very vulnerable. In any case we should pray for them that their indwelling Lord may take full possession of them, as they yield to Him in total surrender.

2. Healing—Experiences like this may leave behind marks and scars, and these can be very deep and take time to heal. It is the experience of many who have been set free from a bondage, or had an evil spirit cast out of them, that they experience a sense of numbness and depression. It can almost seem an anti-climax after the initial joy of release which may have been experienced. We need to pray for the healing of the memories and the binding up of these wounds.

The after-care of people delivered from bondages and other forms of satanic attack is most important. They should be regularly prayed for and constantly encouraged. From time to time they will need fellowship and advice.

The pain that follows is not unlike that which is experienced after an operation. Surgery can be painful, and this ministry is like it. Corrie ten Boom illustrates it in a very helpful manner. When you stop ringing church bells, although you are no longer pulling on the ropes they will continue to sound for a little while longer. So those who have been ministered to may well continue to experience the after-effects of the devil's invasion or siege. They will be tempted at times to believe he is still there, and the bondage remains. The bell still rings. They must "let go of the rope" and trust our Lord entirely. Their whole nervous system has become so used to the presence of this power that it continues for a time to haunt them, as if it is still there after all. But it has gone, and faith believes this, even though feelings contradict faith. But given time, complete dedication of the life and persevering faith, the full healing will follow.

3. Self-discipline—Of course, self-effort itself will not avail in our struggle against satanic power. We always lose that battle. Nevertheless the Lord does require wholehearted cooperation and a genuine desire to be freed. If a person, for example, has been delivered from alcoholism, he may still be tempted to return to his drinking habits. If he continues to frequent bars and public houses, and keeps a large stock of liquor in his house, he may well be back before long into the same bondage. There must be the self-discipline to cut with the past and to avoid, as far as is humanly possible, any possible source of temptation. A person who normally leads a disciplined life will be in a stronger position to resist the inevitable counter-attack of Satan than the person who is slack and self-indulgent. Human effort and discipline is essential to maintain the ground that has been gained from the enemy.

4. Faith—Jesus said, "whatever you ask in prayer, believe that you receive it, and you will" (Matt. 11:24). The person who has been ministered to should be helped to believe that he has received what has been asked for, even if at the time there are no outward signs. It is not always helpful to say to someone after prayer, "Well, do you feel any different?" Feelings don't count here. Faith does. Our faith will help to strengthen theirs. Let us not in any way sow doubts into their minds. We should encourage them to hold on in faith through the sometimes difficult stages in recovery after ministry.

5. *Praise*—For the work of the Spirit to continue in the person, healing and establishing him in a newly orientated life, it is important to underline the need for complete dedication and an unreserved love for our Lord. The key to lasting victory, especially after deliverance from evil spirits, is not only the shield of faith to repel the enemy, but wholehearted worship and love for Jesus. So God fills the person with such love for Him that there is no room to receive its opposite, or for the self-life to rise up and hinder the walk in the Spirit.

So the battle is won—and the enemy retreats in defeat. We experience, as the disciples did, great elation. "Even the spirits are subject to us in Jesus' name." That is wonderful. But let us give glory to God. Lord Alanbrooke described the work of Sir Winston Churchill in the Second World War as bringing Britain "from the abyss to victory." That is what our Lord Jesus Christ has done for mankind, and to Him be all the glory. As the four and twenty elders in heaven say:

> We give thanks to thee, Lord God almighty, who art and who wast, that thou hast taken thy great power and begun to reign. The nations raged, but thy wrath came, and the time for the dead to be judged, for rewarding they servants, the prophets and saints, And those who fear thy name, both small and great, and for destroying the destroyers of the earth.   Revelation 11:17-18

Epilogue

There are two equal and opposite errors into which our race can fall about the devils. One is to disbelieve in their existence. The other is to believe, and to feel an excessive and unhealthy interest in them. They themselves are equally pleased by both errors and hail a materialist or a magician with the same delight. C.S. Lewis, *The Screwtape Letters*[18]

THE PURPOSE OF THIS BOOK has been to try to steer between the two errors that C.S. Lewis so aptly describes. Its aim has been to express belief in the reality of the unseen powers of Satan, but not to give these powers more credit for evil than is their due. One has tried to maintain a positive and encouraging note of triumph throughout. But of the two errors I fear the magician more than the materialist.

Screwtape Letters was deliberately written to expose Satan's devices to ridicule. As such it has been a brilliant success. But Screwtape might yet have achieved victory if he has got Christians to laugh at him too much, and not to have *acted* on the revelation given through that masterly book. Screwtape might yet be having the last laugh.

Spiritual Warfare approaches the subject in a more serious vein. No doubt Screwtape will be wondering how to deal with it, and writing further letters to his nephew offering advice! His tactics may be these:

(1) Get the book laughed out of court. The anti-supernaturalists might well fall for this one.

(2) Get the book adopted as the textbook of the "super-

supernaturalists," and get them to see devils everywhere and in every person.

(3) Get people to take the subject *too* seriously. This might well be his trump card. Let their joy and serenity be taken away. Fill them with fears. Rob them of a sense of humour. Get them to think all the time of evil, rather than "whatever is true, whatever is honourable, whatever is just, whatever is pure, whatever is lovely, whatever is gracious."

Let us see that Screwtape and all his relations really do lose heart this time.